Bed, Brea
Mississippi Valley

by

Dale Lally

Bed, Breakfast & Bike Mississippi Valley
Copyright 2001 by Dale Lally

Cover: *photos by Dale Lally, design by Jean Sullivan*

Maps: *Richard Widhu*

ISBN: 0-933855-22-2
Library of Congress Control Number: 2001 132004

Also available:
Bed, Breakfast & Bike Midwest
Bed, Breakfast & Bike Northeast
Bed, Breakfast & Bike Western Great Lakes
RIDE GUIDE: Covered Bridges of Ohio
RIDE GUIDE: North Jersey 2nd Edition
RIDE GUIDE: Central Jersey 2nd Edition
RIDE GUIDE: South Jersey 2nd Edition
RIDE GUIDE: New Jersey Mountain Biking
RIDE GUIDE: Mountain Biking in the New York Metro Area
RIDE GUIDE: Hudson Valley New Paltz to Staten Island 2nd Edition
and
Happy Endings by Margaret Logan
The Adventure of Two Lifetimes by Peggy & Brian Goetz

Send for our catalog or visit us at www.anacus.com

Published by

ANACUS PRESS INC.

P.O. Box 156, Liberty Corner, New Jersey 07938

"Ride Guide" and "Bed, Breakfast and Bike" are trademarks of Anacus Press, Inc.

Printed in the United States of America

Contents

Numbers correspond to bullets on the inn locator map on page 14

Acknowledgments

I want to publicly thank God our Father for giving me my bicycle, my motorhome, and the opportunity to make this a spiritual journey.

In addition, I wish to thank the following individuals from the physical world for their help, one way or another, in making this book a reality:

Christian Glazar of Anacus Press, who provided the support and impetus for the journey.

Michael Hamner, owner of French Louisiana Bike Tours, for taking me along on a Wednesday evening ride with the Crescent City Bike Club and providing a general entrée into the New Orleans cycling scene.

Jon Anderson and Nick Smith of St. Francisville, Louisiana, who provided an immense amount of information and assistance about cycling in the St. Francisville area.

Earl Smith, member of the Baton Rouge Bike Club and Director of the West Florida Historical Museum, for information on the Jackson, Louisiana, area.

Bill and Kay Jones for providing reservations for all the inns along the Natchez Trace, including their own: Ridgetop B&B near Hampshire, Tennessee.

Dave Edwards of the Jackson, Mississippi, Visitors Bureau and Jim Parks, Millsaps College Librarian Emeritus, for information on the Jackson, Mississippi, area, particularly the new bypass route.

Paul Marquardt, the retired farmer from Prairie du Rocher, who pointed out the alternate flat route along the Illinois side of the Mississippi River. In his honor I named that route the Marquardt Trail.

Mr. Enthusiasm himself, Denny Ward of Marquand, Missouri, who probably does not even own a bike yet, but is on his way to becoming the "Cookie Man" of Missouri, following in the tradition of June Curry, the "Cookie Lady" in Afton, Virginia.

All the wonderful innkeepers for their hospitality and infectious enthusiasm about the profession of innkeeping and B&B travel in general.

Reservations for all of the New Orleans inns were graciously provided by:

> B&B Inc.
> 1021 Moss Street
> P.O. Box 52257
> New Orleans, LA 70152-2257
> (800) 729-4640
> (504) 488-4640

Preface

This book is based on a two-month RV/bicycle trip from New Orleans to St. Louis during the summer of 1999. The purpose of the trip was to collect data on the road conditions of Adventure Cycling's Great Rivers Route (GRR) as well as evaluate the B&B inns along the route. My principal mode of transportation was a 25' 1984 Champion motor home, nicknamed "Das Boot" after the submarine U-96 from the novel *Das Boot (The Boat)* by Lothar Günther Buchheim.

On the rear of the U-96 I stowed two Specialized bikes, an Expedition road bike and a Stump Jumper mountain bike, both from Specialized. In a word, I was prepared for anything—motorized or Specialized.

Why bed & breakfasts and bikes?

Over the past several years, long distance bicycle touring has grown by leaps and bounds for several reasons, most of which come down to health, environment, and the marketplace.

Healthwise, one of the big advantages of cycling is the fact that just about anyone can do it for most of their lives. It is not unusual to see seniors in their 80s or 90s who have taken up cycling as a replacement for running. If there ever was a fountain of youth machine, it is the bicycle. I have ridden on organized tours where three generations of the same family participated, the grandparents on upright bikes while Mom and Dad ride a tandem pulling a trailer loaded with grandkids.

Rising fuel prices and a growing concern about the environment has led many people to seek a viable alternative to motorized travel.

Finally, the marketplace has played a role. Touring cyclists used to take great pride in going fully loaded from campground to campground, with only an occasional motel stop to get re-acquainted with a real bed and unlimited hot showers. Nowadays bicycle touring has become a bit more upscale. While the campers (including this author) are still many in number, many others wish to combine easy and pleasant touring with visits to motels and romantic B&Bs. One only has to look at Vermont, where bicycle tourism—particularly inn-to-inn touring—brings in more revenue than maple syrup production.

Further in this book you will find short discussions on bicycle touring and B&B travel. With a minor exception I purposely did not go into detail on what gear to take along on a tour. That topic has been covered ad infinitum and may be easily accessed by searching the Internet on "bicycle touring." Two very good bicycle touring web sites are Ken Kifer's Bike Page (www.kenkifer.com/bikepages/touring/) and Ed Noonan's Voyager page (www.voyager.net/tailwinds/).

I also did not dedicate much space to restaurants. One can always ask other cyclists about good restaurants, since the situation changes constantly. The ultimate information providers are, of course, the various innkeepers along the route. Providing concierge services (i.e., information on where to go and what to do) has become a significant part of the profession. All of the innkeepers I encountered on this journey were eager to share their knowledge on the local restaurants and attractions. For example, Pat O'Lee, innkeeper at the Nolan House in Waverly, Tennessee, spent half a day taking me around the countryside showing spots involved with Jesse James, who lived nearby under an alias in the late 1870s. Carolyn Estes, innkeeper at the Wildflowers Farm B&B near Calvert, Kentucky, got out her bike and together we cycled several local loops.

Why the Adventure Cycling route?
When Anacus Press asked me to do a *Bed, Breakfast & Bike* guide to the Mississippi Valley, the choice was obvious. Adventure Cycling's already well-established Great Rivers Route provided a wonderful opportunity to check out the B&Bs along what was for me totally new cycling territory. This was particularly true with the spectacular Natchez Trace—rapidly becoming one

of the country's top bicycle touring destinations. The various inns featured in the book were chosen based on a 40- to 70-mile day. On the other hand, three inns were featured in New Orleans alone. This was done to give the touring cyclist an opportunity to partake of all the city has to offer, from the French Quarter to the Garden District.

While Adventure Cycling's classic Great Rivers Route follows the Mississippi Valley from Muscatine, Iowa, to St. Francisville, Louisiana, this book is confined to the area between St. Louis and New Orleans, a distance of about 1,300 miles. For years, the traffic between New Orleans and St. Francisville was ill-suited for road touring. However, recent developments have changed that situation. The first development was the rather belated discovery that mountain bikes and fat-tired touring bikes can easily manage the trails along the levee tops. Various river communities are now working toward improving their portions of the levee-top trail. One excellent example of this is the paved section between New Orleans and Kenner, 12 miles upriver.

The second development is the Mississippi River Trail.

The Mississippi River Trail (MRT)

Several years ago, the states bordering the lower Mississippi joined together to develop a scenic cycling and driving route from St. Genevieve, Missouri, to New Orleans, a distance of about 1,200 miles using existing roads. The result of that collaboration is the new Mississippi River Trail (MRT). The MRT was designed to remain very close to the river and, thankfully, does include a major part of the Natchez Trace Parkway (NTP). As we go to press, various stages were completed in Arkansas, Missouri, Kentucky, Tennessee, and Mississippi. According to information from the MRT site, signage is still lacking in Illinois and Louisiana at presstime.

While collecting data for this book I actually did encounter MRT road signs, particularly around MM 10 on the Natchez Trace Parkway. Interestingly enough, the MRT does take the new back road route via the Emerald Mound between Natchez and the NTP.

When complete, the MRT promises to be a wonderful comple-
ment to Adventure Cycling's Great Rivers Route, enabling cyclists to make a loop without significant backtracking. For the
latest information on the status of the MRT, contact:

> Mississippi River Trail
> 7777 Walnut Grove Road
> Box 27
> Memphis, TN 38120
> (901) 753-1400
> www.bicyclemrt.org
> mrt@bicyclemrt.org

Why the RV?

Purists might rightfully ask why I did not do this whole thing on
the bike alone. A worthy question which demands an equally
worthy answer.

Given the time available (two months), I could never have completed the research or collected all the data while riding only a
bicycle. Based on the ability to use the motor home to drive the
cycling routes, then use the bike(s) to test out local roads and
write up the data every evening on my laptop, I was able to cover
the distances needed. I also managed to update the Adventure
Cycling maps, find alternative routes around problem areas (the
Marquardt Trail in Illinois), and discover a viable (but unofficial)
extension of the Great Rivers Route (which currently ends in St.
Francisville, Louisiana) into New Orleans. Please note that this
was done entirely of my own volition and without any input or
recognition from Adventure Cycling. I just felt that the time had
come to do something about cycling between Baton Rouge and
New Orleans.

Finally, the expertise gained from years of self-contained bicycle
touring in North America and Europe provided me with the confi-
dence to judge a route as to its suitability for inclusion in this
book.

Why bicycle touring?

While living in Louisville, Kentucky, from 1973 to 1990, I watched the Bikecentennial route evolve from the original Trans America Trail (TAT) from Oregon to Virginia into a vast network of bicycle touring routes spanning the entire country. My original interest in bicycle touring was piqued by riding several Kentucky segments of the Bikecentennial trail and actually encountering touring cyclists along its path. Usually traveling in small groups or solo, for the most part self-contained and looking the worse for wear from weeks on the road, these riders became my heroes. I knew that someday I must follow in their path.

The Bikecentennial (later Adventure Cycling) maps provided many of the details needed to navigate through the boondocks. Thus, beginning in the late '70s, I became a regular user of the Bikecentennial maps, amassing a rather substantial collection. Indeed, just looking at the maps often provided inspiration for new trips. The only thing I found lacking on the maps was a detailed presentation of what lay along the routes. Hopefully, the combination of the Adventure Cycling maps and tour guides (such as this one) dedicated to bicycle touring will help to fill that gap. In addition to using the expertise of the local cycling community to develop local loops around the various inns, I regularly supplemented local input with DeLorme's Street Atlas and county maps.

Why me?

In the 1970s I began riding regularly with the Louisville Wheelmen. After completing RAGBRAIs IX and XI across Iowa, I lived and breathed long distance touring. Subsequently, two wonderful opportunities for exotic touring presented themselves in 1975 and again in 1978, when I took students from the University of Louisville on bicycle tours through Austria, France, Germany, and Switzerland. (In the early '60s I had been stationed in Europe as a German linguist for the USAF, and taking the students to Europe was like returning home.) On six different occasions from 1980 to 1990 I cycled throughout Europe, from the south of England to France and along the Rhine in Holland and Germany. In 1990, I moved to bicycle heaven, otherwise known as northern New York, specifically the St. Lawrence Valley. There I had the great fortune to join the Canton Bicycle Club, which provided just the right opportunity to host two major cycling events on behalf of the League of American Bicyclists (GEAR '92 and GEAR '97 and two Elder Hostels, and to start writing about cycling.

There, in the Valley of the St. Lawrence, touching two great nations, America and Canada, everything began coming together. The thousands of miles I had cycled throughout Ontario, Quebec, New York, and Vermont—sometimes alone but more often in the wonderful company of riders from the Canton Bicycle Club—were soon translated into articles and the first book. In retrospect, I now see that those nine short years in northern New York were indeed the stepping off point for a writing career about the outdoors, a career that will apparently take me all over North America and hopefully abroad.

What about the future?
Bicycle touring—particularly the inn-to-inn sort—is not only alive and well, but growing by leaps and bounds. Not particularly content to just ride from inn to inn, many riders will now ship their bikes to the various inns and bike around the area. Others combine both modes of touring by driving to an inn, and then cycling to the various neighboring inns. The combinations are practically endless. Furthermore, thanks to the the slow but sure progress of the Mississippi River Trail, the touring possibilities in the Mississippi Valley are about to take a quantum leap forward.

Because of the nature of touring on mostly back roads, this trip led me to encounter delightful people and out-of-the-way places. Whether driving the motor home or testing out route segments on my bike, every morning I looked forward to my next discovery. That is probably the greatest joy of bicycle touring—it combines a sense of adventure and discovery, and provides a vehicle to meet wonderful people, even if it's just for a short meeting on the side of the road to compare notes. You might start out meeting strangers, but end up making friends.

Finally, those hours spent in the saddle provided me with wonderful opportunities for introspection and finding joy in the world in which we live. From a bicycle, one can see, smell, taste, feel, and hear God talking in a manner not possible when riding around the countryside encased in a metal box with wheels.

I hope that each and every one of you can experience better communication with your inner selves and with this glorious world in the same manner that I did. I wish you a sincere *Namasté* and "Tailwinds."

Dale Lally
Pompano Beach, Florida
March, 2001

The author and U-96

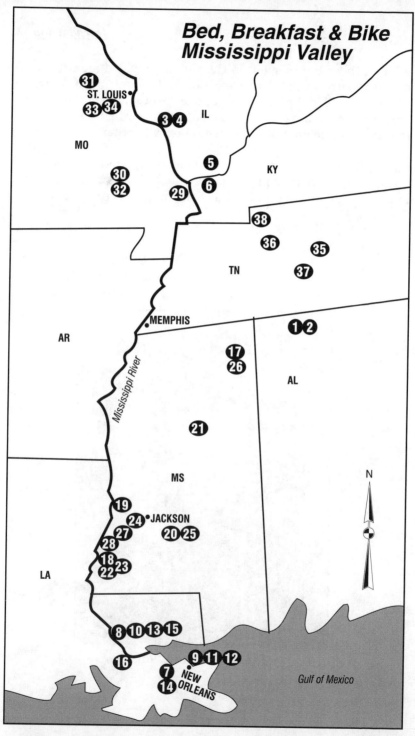

Bullet numbers on map correspond to inns in the Table of Contents

How to Use This Book

Information About the B&Bs

When it comes to B&Bs, no two establishments are alike. They all reflect the individual styles and tastes of their owners. Nevertheless, virtually everyone will find something that tickles their fancy in the selected cyclist-friendly accommodations in this book, from gentrified farms to traditional B&Bs to mountaintop lodges. Some are popular because of their setting, some because of their rich history or distinct architecture. The entry for each inn contains descriptions of ambiance, amenities, and locale to guide your selection.

From a management and hospitality perspective, the lodgings fall, in general, into two different categories: B&Bs, which tend to be smaller, family-run businesses where the innkeeper will greet you at the door and serve you breakfast, and inns, which are somewhat larger establishments with larger staffs and slightly less personal—albeit hospitable and professional—service. If you're the kind of person who can't live without a TV, phone, and mini-bar in your room and who must have porters, fax machines, and room service on-demand, you probably won't enjoy a stay at a small, intimate, relaxed B&B or inn.

That said, many B&Bs and small inns are adding amenities, such as in-room phones with voicemail or internet access, and some may even offer a television or a mini-bar in your room. In any event, if there is an amenity that you can't live without it's best to check with the innkeeper before booking a room. Many establishments also have non-smoking policies, so if you're a smoker ask about the smoking policy when you make a reservation.

The heading for each listing includes all contact information, including Web addresses where available, plus rate information. The rate description is based on the rates when I visited the inns and is subject to change. Rather than give a specific rate, which can quickly become obsolete, I have instead placed the rates in a range as follows:

Budget:	$90 or less
Moderate:	$91-140
Deluxe:	$141-199
Luxury:	$200 and up

Cycling & Maps

Besides the Adventure Cycling Great Rivers Route that ties this book together, there are also local routes originating at many of the inns. Maps and cue sheets for these local tours are provided. In many cases, innkeepers or local bike shops can make additional recommendations.

In addition, the heading for each inn contains a reference to the appropriate Adventure Cycling maps (where applicable) in the upper right-hand corner. "GR" refers to the Great Rivers Route; "TAT" refers to the Trans-America Trail, and "ST" refers to the Southern Tier Route.

Descriptions of each ride address terrain, road and traffic conditions, as well as interesting sites and landmarks along the way. The author rode a touring bike with 700 x 35 tires on all routes. However, where road conditions are better suited to either a mountain or hybrid bike it's noted.

The ride cues are well documented and mapped; however, it is a good idea to carry a detailed county map. Often innkeepers will have them on hand; otherwise, they usually can be found at a local gas station, convenience store, bike shop, outdoor recreation or book store, or through a tourist bureau or chamber of commerce. In some areas, maps especially designed for cyclists are available and are included in the section on additional resources. In a few instances, free maps are available from local real estate offices.

Before You Go

Safety First
No activity is completely predictable and/or safe—bicycle touring included. However, one can take certain measures to decrease the possibility for disaster on a bicycle tour. The most important is to visualize a safe trip. Do not dwell on disaster. Before your departure, thank the Universe for a safe trip.

You should also take a few precautions:

Be highly visible. For me this means having as much of the color of yellow as possible, which extends to my panniers and water bottles. This will give approaching motorists and truckers sufficient warning to pass safely.

Wear a helmet. I am a firm believer in helmets, mainly because I have landed on one at least twice in my life. On the first occasion I tangled with a kid chasing a Frisbee in a park. He did not hear me, and I sure did not see him until it was too late. I flew right over the handlebar and landed on my helmet with no injuries. On the second occasion, the bike slipped out from under me in a rainstorm (in the same park!) and down I went. In neither instance were cars involved. I would not have written this book had I not been faithfully wearing my helmet.

Use a rear-view mirror. This safety device is a huge bone of contention among many riders; many say just look around. Obviously, looking around and being constantly aware of your environment is a good practice—if you are limber enough and have developed the ability to quickly glance over your shoulder. There is, however, another element to this equation: motorists. In my experience, if motorists *know* you are aware of their presence—or, more importantly, if they *feel* you are watching them in the mirror—they are usually rather accommodating. In my pre-mirror days I often noticed that some motorists liked to "sneak up" on me, come dangerously close, lean on the horn, and then roar off. But after I began using a bar end mirror, they could see me watching them—or they *thought* I was watching them—which very often defused the situation rather effectively. The rider's task is to give passing drivers the impression that you are watching them constantly; that can be effectively done with a rear view mirror. Not just one of those small helmet-mounted mirrors, but a big mirror easily seen by the drivers. The advice to not depend completely on your mirrors is very true. But the combination of a big mirror and looking around should cover all your bases. This leads to another safety device.

Pack a cell phone or something that looks like a cell phone. (I usually carry a cell phone and/or my amateur two meter transceiver.) Should you have a catastrophic breakdown or find yourself being harassed by drivers on a lonely back road, stopping on the side of the road, whipping out the cell phone, and making a big production of writing down a license plate number or calling the police will usually cause road bullies to clear out of the area fast.

Beware of loose dogs. They seem to be everywhere in countryside, and can be quite intimidating. I suggest carrying a can of HALT as a last resort, just in case yelling *"No!"* or *"Go home!"* has little effect.

What to Take
This is a topic that has been cussed and discussed ad infinitum. There are many lists available on the net; check out Ken Kifer's Bike Pages at www.kenkifer.com or Ed Noonan'sVoyager site at www.voyager.net/tailwinds. What makes this tour a bit unique is the remoteness of some of the segments, particularly in northwest Tennessee and southeast Missouri, which calls for packing a few extra rations and water.

Another aspect is the season. Avoid the hot summer. This leaves spring and fall—obviously the prettiest times of the year, but also the seasons where you may encounter rather stark temperature swings. After a beautiful seventy-five-degree late autumn day, the morning temperature could drop into the 30s. To handle possible cold weather, I suggest packing at least one complete polypropylene outfit starting with sock liners, upper and lower underwear, glove liners, and ski cap. This entire outfit will take up precious little room in the panniers, weigh less than four pounds, and do double duty as pajamas. Avoid clothing items made of cotton, which retains moisture. If riding exclusively in cool or cold weather, good old-fashioned wool is a good choice. But for big daily temperature swings, polypropylene or any one of the new lightweight fabrics would be the material of choice.

—Important Disclaimer—

While this book provides as accurate a description of these rides as possible, road conditions and other critical information provided in these pages can change overnight. It is your own responsibility to have a thorough understanding of the routes you ride, the mechanical condition of your bike, and your riding ability. By purchasing this book or borrowing it from a friend, you have released Anacus Press, the authors, and the artists from any liability for injuries you may sustain while using this book as a guide.

A Primer for the B&B Traveler

B&B travel is simply wonderful. If you just need a room to get in out of the weather, then what you want is a cheap motel. But if you want to be pampered at every step, if you enjoy sitting around of an evening chatting with other guests, sleeping in a fourposter bed, and stuffing yourself on a scrumptious breakfast, then you are a prime candidate for B&B travel.

Historic bed & breakfasts are popular because of their personal and non-commercial qualities. The site is usually a restored, older home with an average of six guestrooms, located in a village setting, usually on the fringe of a large metropolitan area. Their charm often lies in this "off-the-beaten-path" location, allowing guests to immerse themselves in the history and wonders of days gone by.

Because B&Bs are almost always owner-occupied, the innkeeper is often available to share information on local folklore and tradition. He or she can also recommend walking trails, point you to antique shops, and is knowledgeable about the best spots to sample the local cuisine. This personal touch is another reason why bed & breakfasts have become so popular.

Ivonne Cuendet, a veteran innkeeper and member of the Professional Association of Innkeepers International, offers the following suggestions to make your stay at any inn a pleasant one:

1. Reservations are always recommended, particularly since the majority of B&Bs have a limited number of accommodations.

2. Check-in times are often limited since many of the innkeepers might be absent during the day running errands or working a second job. If you discover that you will be late arriving, give them a call. (Every innkeeper I have ever met was very tolerant with bicycle tourists.)

3. Advance payment is often required to guarantee a reservation. Along this line, a cancellation policy of 4 to 7 days is usually

in effect. While on the surface this might appear to be a bit hard-nosed, you must remember that that room might represent anywhere from twenty to thirty percent of available accommodations. A last minute cancellation could represent a substantial loss to the inn.

4. If you find it necessary to ask for directions to the inn, always make it clear that you are arriving by bicycle since most innkeepers deal with guests arriving by automobile. This is very important since safe access to an out-of-the-way inn might be totally different for bicycle tourists. For example, Bill and Kay Jones, owner/innkeepers of the Ridgetop B&B near Hohenwald, Tennessee, often instruct cyclists to approach their inn from the rear, or Ridgetop Road. More often than not they will offer to tote arriving cyclists up to the hill with their pickup.

5. While breakfast in one form or another is always complimentary, it is often served at specific times—often far too late for touring cyclists. Since most cyclists like to be on the road right around sunrise, an early breakfast is often desirable. With proper notice, most innkeepers can arrange for an early serving. However, due to the schedules of kitchen help, some inns might not be able to provide an early full breakfast. In those few instances, a light continental breakfast is usually set out for early risers. It is always prudent to mention the need for an early breakfast when making reservations.

6. When making reservations, ask about bicycle storage. Due to a preponderance of expensive rugs and antiques, many innkeepers are reluctant to permit bikes in rooms. Even in the case of a secluded B&B where theft is highly improbable, it is always prudent to ask about secure stowage.

To Ivonne's list, I would add the following:

7. Internet access: For many touring cyclists, it is necessary to keep in touch with home. In addition, many cyclists like to keep a journal of the day's events and e-mail it home. The introduction of small palm-sized computers/communications devices have

enabled tourists to do both via the internet. Many innkeepers now provide some sort of connection. Some, like the Lanaux House and The Chimes, offer total access via private, in-room phone connections, while others provide extremely limited access via the house phone. Some provide no access whatsoever.

The presence (or absence) of in-room, private phone/fax connections is often a function of the innkeeper's ideas on the experience offered their guests. Many guests wish to be cut off from all electronic communications during their visit while others cannot stand to be away from the Internet for more than half a day. If you do encounter a modular phone jack in your room with no phone attached, check with the innkeeper before connecting your equipment. The presence of a phone jack with no phone may be a sign that that line is one of the main numbers of the inn. Spending an extended time surfing the 'net in effect cuts off the inn from incoming reservations. The best approach is to get on, get your mail, and get off.

8. Using laundry facilities: At the end of the day, bicycle tourists always need to change into clean shorts and jerseys. Experienced riders usually take one spare set along. Thus it is necessary to wash your cycling togs often. While all of the innkeepers I asked about laundry facilities were more than willing to let their cycling guests refresh their shorts and jerseys, out of courtesy this should be done in the evening after all of the linens from the inn have been washed.

Useful Web Sites for B&B Travelers
www.bedandbreakfast.com
www.bbonline.com

All About New Orleans

New Orleans, Louisiana, also known as NOLA, Crescent City, or the Big Easy, certainly has it all: great entertainment, great restaurants, great scenery, and great bed & breakfasts. The B&Bs operate under a few odd restrictions—one of them being that they cannot serve hot meals. Therefore, forget about a full breakfast in any New Orleans B&B. However, all of the reviewed B&Bs are allowed to serve a continental breakfast, and most of the upscale inns take this as far as they are allowed. For instance, the Chimes and Maison Marigny serve "gourmet" continental breakfasts, which are vastly more elaborate than the standard coffee and pastries. At the Lanaux House, each guestroom is equipped with a microwave oven and small refrigerator stuffed with breakfast goodies, including chocolate-filled croissants! Certainly, the guest must not be shy about asking to use the kitchen or the laundry. Just about every innkeeper I met stressed that one of their major goals was to make the guests feel at home, and that included use of the whole house.

Another rule concerns alcoholic beverages. In addition to the stricture on hot meals, none of the B&Bs reviewed for this book may sell alcoholic beverages—such as wine to go with cheese—due to the absence of a very expensive liquor license. But since you are a guest in their home, the innkeeper may *share* a glass of wine or two with you, provided they don't charge you for it.

Cycling in New Orleans

While New Orleans enjoys a reputation as a quirky, fun-loving city, cycling has a *different* image altogether. With vast numbers of cars and delivery trucks competing for space and equally vast numbers of visitors all tramping about the narrow streets bearing names like Bourbon, Dauphine, and Chartres, cycling can be a bit of a challenge. Following are a few observations on cycling in New Orleans:

1. For the most part, the city's narrow streets, stuffed with parked cars and open doors, constitute a very serious safety problem. Thus it is best to avoid cycling in the French Quarter, at least on the weekend when it is packed with tourists. This is one of the very few instances where I have noticed that walking is vastly better and more exciting than driving or cycling. Within the French Quarter, there is just too much to see, hear, and smell and the potential for bike accidents is truly phenomenal.

2. Except for early morning on the weekends, there is always extremely heavy traffic on every major thoroughfare, as well as many secondary roads.

3. With notable exceptions, New Orleans drivers appear to be somewhat unyielding to cyclists, particularly when trying to pass you on such streets as Esplanade Avenue.

4. The narrow city streets are generally in horrible condition, with huge potholes everywhere, even in the finest of neighborhoods. Furthermore, these breaks in the pavement are very often right at the junction of the driving and parking lanes. Thus, in addition to watching for open doors and passing traffic, one must also watch for these huge potholes. Avoiding them means pulling further out to the left and into the traffic, which is already very close. It is imperative for cyclists to constantly check ahead for these sometimes monstrous breaks. This high state of vigilance also means that, in order to fully enjoy the scenery, you might wish to dismount and push your bike through some areas.

5. Street signs seem to be a problem, probably because every tourist and college kid wants to take one home as a souvenir. While doing research for this book, I often had difficulty finding street signs.

Having said all this, I still wish to encourage everyone to try bicycle touring around New Orleans. The overall beauty and ambience are simply too fantastic to ignore. I am convinced that—with the exception of the French Quarter—only from a bicycle can you really partake of the city's atmosphere.

Two Suggested Tours

Both local tours begin and end at centrally located Jackson Square. The estimated times to completion are *not* based on mileage, but rather on the scenery and restaurants along the way. The tours were also designed with the intent of allowing the rider to complete shorter loops.

In addition to tours original to this book, check out Michael Hamner's page (http://freeman.sob.tulane.edu/bike/mikepage.htm) for more New Orleans tours and information.

NOLA Local Tour #1
The Garden District Historic Neighborhood and Audubon Park Loop

Distance: Approximately 11 miles.
Estimated time to complete this tour: Give yourself at least five hours.

This whole area should be your first choice for a scenic, unstructured, self-guided tour within the city. It is an easy ride from the Central Business District/French Quarter. In addition to continuous magnificent views of classic New Orleans architecture and gardens, you will also have the opportunity to take a spin around Audubon Park.

0.0　　From the Café du Monde at the intersection of St. Ann and Decatur, proceed south on Decatur, which becomes Magazine Street as it crosses Canal Street.

1.5　　Turn right onto Erato and then left onto Coliseum. After a few blocks you will be literally in the midst of the Garden District. Once there, take your time, cruise up and down all the back streets, enjoy the magnificent gardens and homes—and smell the roses. To visit Audubon Park, continue west on Coliseum.

4.0　　At the T intersection where Coliseum Street ends, turn right onto Henry Clay for one block to Perrier and then left into Audubon Park. After a spin around the 2.3-mile bike path, you may retrace the route or take Tschoupitoulas back to the French quarter.

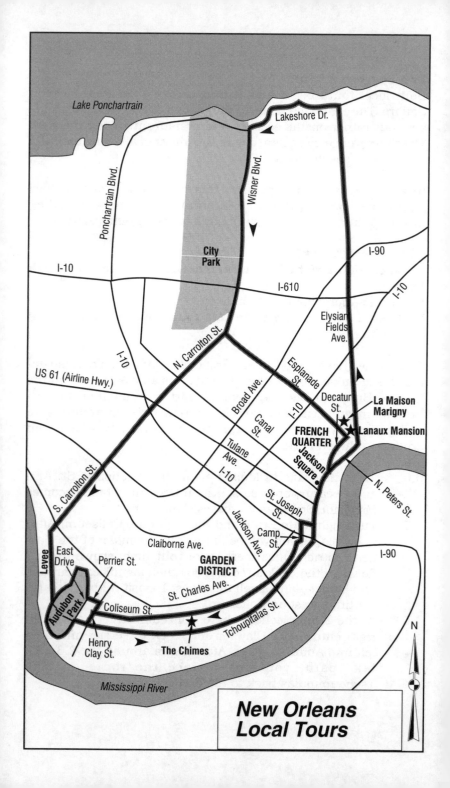

NOLA Local Tour #2
Lake Ponchartrain Beach Loop Length
Distance: 13.5 to 23 miles
Estimated time to complete this loop: Three to five hours, depending on the options chosen

This tour will take you out Elysian Fields Avenue to Lake Ponchartrain Beach and along the edge of City Park and Bayou St. John. At the intersection of Wisner Boulevard, North Carrollton, and Esplanade Street (mile 11.0), you will have the option of returning to the French Quarter via Esplanade Street (13.5 miles) or of taking the longer route home via Carrollton Street, the levee, and Audubon Park (23 miles).

0.0   From Jackson Square, proceed northeast on Decatur for about three blocks and then bear right onto North Peters for just a couple of blocks to where it ends at Elysian Fields Avenue.
0.5   Bear left and remain on Elysian Fields Avenue.
7.0   At the T intersection turn left onto Lakeshore Drive.
8.0   Right into Cloverleaf Drive, which will bring you back around and underneath Lakeshore Drive and onto Beauregard Avenue South.
11.0   Decision time: Bearing left onto Esplanade Street will bring you back to the French Quarter for a total distance of 14 miles. Bearing right onto North Carrollton will take you to the levee and Audubon Park for a total of 23 glorious miles.

Option 1—bear left onto Esplanade.

13.0   Right onto Decatur.
13.5   Arrive at starting point in Jackson Square. Oh, yes—remember to stop off at the Café du Monde for bignettes and coffee.

Option 2—The levee and Audubon Park

11.0   Bear right onto North Carrollton Street

15.0   At the intersection of South Carrollton and St. Charles (mile 15.0), you will have the option of turning left onto St. Charles for a more direct return to the French Quarter (21 miles) or continuing straight to the levee and following it around to the left to Tschoupitoulas. This will bring you back to the French Quarter for a total of 23 miles.

Note: If you have time for lunch or dinner, check out La Madeleine Deli near the intersection of St. Charles and South Carrollton Street. Just a few hundred yards from the paved bike path that runs for twelve miles along the top of the levee out to Kenner, Louisiana, La Madeleine is a favorite haunt of the Crescent City Bicycle Club, particularly following the Wednesday evening ride along the levee.

New Orleans Cycling Resources
Before you go cycling anywhere in New Orleans, check with Bicycle Michael's, 622 Frenchmen Street, (504) 945-9505. Everyone in the shop is a rider and good source of information on where and how to cycle in the Crescent City. In order to get you into the proper mood for this most French of American cities, Michael can even chat with you in French.

Another great source for local New Orleans and Louisiana info in general is Michael Hamner, owner of French Louisiana Bicycle Tours (www.flbt.com). As far as I know, FLBT is the only bicycle tour company native to Louisiana. It was Michael who introduced me to the Crescent City Bicycle Club (http://home.gnofn.org/~cyclists). His personal home page (http://freeman.sob.tulane.edu/bike/mikepage.htm) is a treasure trove of info on cycling in the Big Easy.

For New Orleans bicycle shops and/or contacts refer to the Appendix/Useful addresses.

For the Lanaux House and La Maison Marigny, Bicycle Michael's and the French Quarter Bike Shop on Dumaine Street are the closest bicycle shops. For the Chimes, it's Herwig's Bicycle Store. GNO (Greater New Orleans) Cycles is around mile 14 of the 23-mile local loop.

Surviving New Orleans on a Bicycle

1. Wear a helmet! Wear a helmet! Wear a helmet!

2. Use a mirror! Use a mirror! Use a mirror! Not just any mirror but one sufficiently large enough to give motorists the clear impression you are watching them constantly. In general, drivers become very civil when they think they are being watched. Passing motorists usually cannot see the small helmet- or glasses-mounted mirrors and very often think they can get away with something.

3. Get a good, detailed map.

4. Be adventurous and be prepared to stop and explore. There are literally hundreds of exotic restaurants and shops nestled in out-of-the-way places. However, in case you might spend some time away from the bicycle, remember to secure it with a very sturdy lock.

5. If possible, establish contact with the Crescent City Bicycle Club (http://home.gnofn.org/~cyclists) prior to arrival and check their ride schedule. Going on a club ride will provide a good introduction and frame of reference to cycling in the city.

Directions to the New Orleans Inns

Lanaux House (by bike from the levee)
If approaching New Orleans by bicycle along the eastern shore levee from Baton Rouge, work your way downriver to just past Audubon Park. One of the first major streets will be Tchoupitoulas Street. Turn onto Tchoupitoulas towards the downtown area and after two blocks turn left (north) onto Henry Clay. After five blocks on Clay you will cross Magazine Street. Continue north on Clay for three blocks to Coliseum. Turn right onto Coliseum East, which will twist and turn but still provide a pleasant, low-traffic path into the downtown area. FYI, as you proceed inbound on Coliseum, you will pass directly by the Chimes B&B at the intersection of Coliseum and Constantinople.

Coliseum joins with Camp Street just before you reach the big Crescent City bridge. Turning left onto Camp will bring you into the downtown area. *Caution:* Shortly after passing under the big bridge, at the very first light there could be a lot of rather fast traffic on your right exiting off the bridge. If heavy traffic does not bother you, stay on Camp Street, which becomes Chartres, and *voila*, you are in the French Quarter, a one-hundred-block area of world-class restaurants, night life, shops and ... unusual characters. At the far end of the Quarter, Chartres intersects with Esplanade, the location of the Lanaux House.

If you prefer to avoid most of the traffic (completely avoiding traffic in New Orleans is impossible!), continue on Camp past the bridge for two blocks and take a right onto St. Joseph. Take St. Joseph for three blocks to Annunciation and turn left. Annunciation eventually becomes North Peters, then Decatur, then North Peters again. Finally, just beyond the French Market, you will run into Esplanade to your left.

Lanaux House (by car from I-10)
If approaching the Lanaux House by car from I-10, the easiest way to find it is to get off the interstate at exit 237 onto Highway 46 (Elysian Fields) and continue south for 1.3 miles to where it ends at North Peters Street. Bear right onto North Peters for one short block and then right again onto Esplanade Street. The Lanaux House will be on your right at the intersection with Chartres Street, barely two tenths of a mile from your last turn onto Esplanade.

La Maison Marigny
The directions to La Maison Marigny are almost identical to the Lanaux House for both bicycle and automobile travelers. Merely continue west on Esplanade for two blocks to Bourbon Street. Take a right onto Bourbon and La Maison Marigny will be the first small house one half block down on your right. According to the owners, it is the only B&B on Bourbon Street.

The Chimes (by bike from the levee)
Follow the same directions for the Lanaux House and La Maison Marigny but with a minor difference. Long before you reach the downtown area you will find The Chimes on your right at the intersection of Coliseum and Constantinople.

The Chimes (by car from I-10)
From exit 233, follow the streetcar tracks south along South Carrollton for three miles around to St. Charles. Once on St. Charles, continue to follow the tracks for 2.7 miles to Constantinople Street. Turn right onto Constantinople for four blocks to Coliseum. The Chimes will be the first house on your right, after the intersection of Constantinople and Coliseum Streets.

Parking in New Orleans
Lanaux House and La Maison Marigny: This is obviously a non-issue for bicycles. However, should someone be bringing you into the city by car to start your tour, or picking you up afterwards, parking could be a problem. For the Lanaux House and La Maison Marigny, this is particularly the case since they are both very close to the Quarter and offer only on-street parking.

On the other hand, the Chimes is a stroll of just a few blocks from the St. Charles streetcar line. In this case, park your vehicle as close as possible to the B&B and forget it in favor of taking the St. Charles streetcar or Magazine Street bus into town.

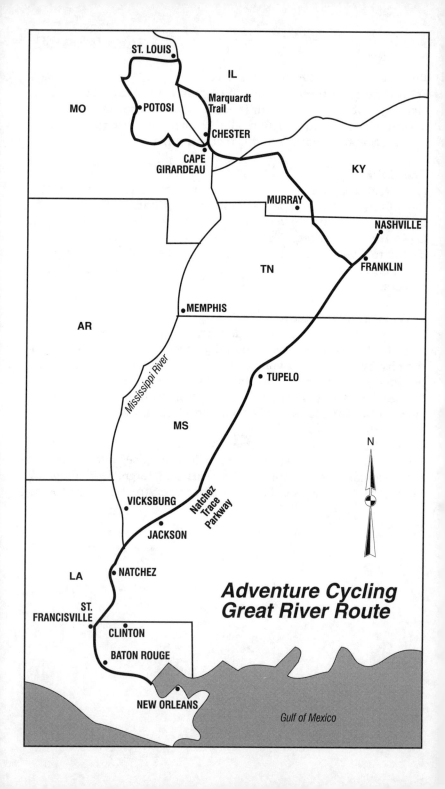

The Great Rivers Route
Including the Natchez Trace Parkway

While the complete span of Adventure Cycling's classic Great Rivers Route lies between Muscatine, Iowa, and St. Francisville, Louisiana, this book will cover only the segment between St. Francisville and St. Louis, Missouri, a total distance of about 1,200 miles. Since many bicycle tourists will want to begin or end their tour in New Orleans—like St. Louis, a city that offers easy access to all forms of public transportation including air, bus, and rail—it was decided to extend the coverage of *Bed, Breakfast & Bike Mississippi Valley* to include an unofficial extension of the route from St. Francisville to New Orleans, for a grand total of about 1,300 miles. Riding the alternative Marquardt Trail through Prairie du Rocher shortens the distance between St. Louis and New Orleans to about 1,100 miles.

Where do you want to go today? East or west bank?
One of the very first questions asked about cycling into or out of New Orleans concerns which side of the river is best. Except for the twelve miles of paved levee path between New Orleans and Kenner, both sides are of essentially equal quality and construction—unpaved crushed rock. Since both New Orleans and Baton Rouge are on the east bank, there is generally less traffic on the west bank. The real question is: Where do you want to go?

If your destination is Baton Rouge, remain on the east bank. Keep in mind that, if you do remain on the east bank, the only recommended accommodation between New Orleans and Baton Rouge is the Tezcuco Plantation, near Darrow, Louisiana, just about half way between New Orleans and Baton Rouge.

For northbounders continuing on to St. Francisville and beyond, the west bank route through Vacherie, Donaldsonville, Plaquemine, Grosse Tete, and New Roads—completely avoiding Baton Rouge—is recommended. Here you will have the opportunity to cycle pleasant back roads and have your choice of several fine B&B inns. Furthermore, cycling the west bank will also provide easy access to the (haunted?) Gatorland bike shop in Plaquemine, the only bike shop on the west bank before Natchez.

Once the northbound rider reaches St. Francisville, Louisiana, the Great Rivers Route remains east of the Mississippi, eventually recrossing it via the very narrow bridge at Cape Girardeau, Missouri. However, if you decide to forego the Missouri hills and ride the alternate Marquardt Trail, you will remain on the east side of the Mississippi all the way into East St. Louis, Illinois. At that point, you may, with unsullied honor, take the bike onto the Metro and cross the river into St. Louis proper.

Northbound or southbound?
Another question, of course, is whether to cycle this route from south to north or vice versa. The prevailing wind could play a minor role in determining the direction of travel. During the spring and summer, the prevailing winds are from south to north. Sometime in October, the winds shift around from the North. The ideal times to ride any part of this route are either in the spring or the autumn, when the heat abates and the evenings are cool. Going from south to north will tend to keep the sun out of your eyes. However, the north-to-south route will allow you to start out in the warm days of spring or autumn and follow the warm weather to the south. The research for this book was done from south to north.

Overall terrain
The terrain along the Great River Route goes from absolutely tabletop flat between New Orleans and New Roads, Louisiana, to a series of killer hills in southeast Missouri. Over the past 30 years of cycling, I have certainly experienced bigger hills, but not in this quantity. On the back roads between Cape Girardeau and St. Louis, I encountered one white-knuckle hill after another. Not only were they extremely steep, with twists and turns and

less than zero visibility, but the local dump and logging trucks were hurtling along with nary a thought about encountering any other traffic, least of all touring cyclists. That Missouri segment of the Great Rivers Route was, without a doubt, the absolute toughest cycling I have ever encountered. But those are not the only hills. Between Waverly, Tennessee, and Cave-in-Rock, Illinois, you will also encounter many granny-gear hills. Fortunately, motor vehicle traffic along that stretch was rather sparse, with few big trucks in evidence. Having said all that, I wish to point out that the most notable and friendly encounters with hospitable folks along the whole tour took place in Missouri.

For northbounders, the steepest hill of all (excluding the front driveway to the Ridgetop B&B) was a short but nasty climb out of the Ohio River valley northwest of Birdsville, Kentucky, along SR 763 (AC: GR II, 19). For heavily-laden southbounders, this downhill will be a total white-knuckle experience. That hill was so steep I had serious reservations about U-96's ability to climb it.

Alternatives to the AC Great Rivers Route
As we went to press, the official starting/ending point for Adventure Cycling's Great Rivers Route was in St. Francisville, Louisiana. As explained above, this book follows an extended route all the way from New Orleans to the Gateway Arch in St. Louis, Missouri. Due to several difficult areas encountered during the trip, I went off the Great Rivers Route looking for viable alternatives. This was true in the case of short segments near Jackson, Louisiana; Natchez, Mississippi; and a rather extensive alternative route between East St. Louis, Illinois, and Ft. Kaskaskia, Illinois. (The Marquardt Trail, page 200, named after the retired farmer from Prairie du Rocher, Illinois, who pointed out the route turn by turn.)

The Great Rivers Route—divided into manageable segments
In order to enable cyclists to complete this tour either in incre-
ments or all at once, this route is divided into four segments: 1)
New Orleans to Natchez, Mississippi; 2) Natchez to Nashville; 3)
Nashville to St. Louis; and 4) an alternative—and flat—route along
the Illinois side of the Mississippi River from Ft. Kaskaskia into
St. Louis, Missouri, via East St. Louis, Illinois.

**Segment One—between New Orleans and Natchez (220 miles)—
Levees, Bridges, and Ferries**

Levees
Between New Orleans and St. Francisville, there are only two
viable route options. I recommend following the Mississippi along
the pancake-flat trail on top of the levee. The other option—US
61, or Airline Highway—has a wide, paved shoulder, but the extremely heavy traffic and unyielding drivers make this route somewhat unpleasant.

For all practical purposes, this unofficial extension of the Great
Rivers Route begins and ends at the intersection of South
Carrollton and St. Charles Avenues in New Orleans. There you
will find a wonderful, multi-use trail on top of the levee, paved for
at least twelve miles out past the town of Kenner. The trail parallels River Road, which is almost always in sight from the top of
the levee. Unfortunately, the closer to the city, the more traffic
you will encounter on River Road. Thus, it is best to ride the
levee as much as possible. Occasionally the trail will be blocked
by industrial sites, making it necessary to detour onto the road.
Though these detours are usually less than a mile in length, be
sure to exercise extreme caution, wear a helmet, be highly visible, and use a mirror.

While there is normally not much traffic away from the city, what
traffic there is usually consists of big trucks trundling between
the local industrial sites. One such location will be the Bonne
Carre spillway, about 25 miles out. Designed to drain excess water
from Lake Ponchartrain into the Mississippi, the narrow, two-

lane road traversing the spillway is actually below the lake level. On occasion—usually in the spring when the lake is high—it might be intentionally flooded to equalize water levels between Lake Pontchartrain and the Mississippi River.

After Bonne Carre, northbounders should continue on top of the levee to Reserve and cross over the river via the Edgard ferry, about 33 miles out. Southbounders will remain on this the eastern side of the river all the way into New Orleans. (Due to the lack of bicycle-friendly bridges, the only consistently practical way to cross the Mississippi in Louisiana is via the ferries.) Should you arrive when the Edgard ferry is not operating (during the summer of 1999, it did not operate on the weekends!) then you must continue another eight miles on the east bank to the Veterans' Memorial Bridge to cross the river. If successful in crossing the river via the Edgard ferry, northbounders are now on the west bank of the river. Get back up on top of the levee at the first opportunity and head for Vacherie. North of Donaldsonville, all levee riding will give way to road riding.

Crossing the Mississippi River, Louisiana-style
In Louisiana, crossing the Mississippi River can be a bit frustrating for bicycle tourists. While the various New Orleans ferries take care of the problem in that area, further upriver towards St. Francisville, the situation deteriorates rather dramatically. One must be familiar with the ferry and bridge situations, each of which has its own particular hurdles to conquer.

Ferries
Following are the schedules for the ferries at Edgard, White Castle, Plaquemine, and St. Francisville. Note the truncated schedules for the Reserve and White Castle ferries, neither of which operate on weekends. In addition, the White Castle ferry does not operate during the day between 8am and 3:30pm. Only the St. Francisville and Plaquemine ferries operate all day, seven days a week.

Reserve to Edgard—5am to 9pm, M-F, every ½ hour.

White Castle—5am to 8am and 3:30pm to 7:30pm, M-F, every ½ hour.

Plaquemine—5am to 9pm, seven days, every ½ hour.

St Francisville to New Roads—4am to midnight, seven days, every ½ hour.

Note: Ferry schedules are subject to change. For the latest info on the Louisiana ferries, contact the Louisiana DOT at www.dotd.state.la.us/about/ferry/schedule.shtml. This is a great site which, among other things, provides links to the departments of transportation of most other states.

Bridges

Unfortunately, the bridge situation is even more difficult. Between New Orleans and the Mississippi line, there is but one bridge that is even remotely bicycle-friendly: the Veterans Memorial Bridge, near Vacherie. The good news is, it has a four-foot-wide paved shoulder that will accommodate cyclists. However, since it is built very high to accommodate large oceangoing ships, it could be very windy at the crest. In addition, it appears that the paved shoulder is seldom—if ever—swept free of tire-eating debris. Finally, the Louisiana DOT has planted reflectors diagonally across the paved shoulder every ten to twenty feet along the entire span. That is the bad news. If you decide to cross that bridge, be prepared to fight the crosswinds, dodge debris, and ride around those reflectors.

In order successfully cross this bridge, I recommend sturdy tires or some sort of patch kit to fix flats. The safest way is to walk the bike. Even though the bridge itself is only about 1.5 miles long with a steep grade, you only have to climb half of that. Once you reach the crest of the span, it's downhill the rest of the way. If you use cleated cycling shoes, remember to bring a pair of walking shoes. If high winds are encountered, it is rather easy to hang onto the bridge railing to keep from being blown out onto the traffic lane. This is a measure I have used on several occasions while riding with the Canton (NY) Bicycle Club across the huge Alexandria Bay Bridge over the St. Lawrence river on the border between New York and Ontario.

If you put off crossing the river at this point, the next bicycle-friendly opportunity to cross the river will be the White Castle ferry, another 45 miles west, which operates on a truncated schedule.

After coming off the Veterans' Bridge, turn onto Highway 18 West and get back up on the levee as soon as possible. It is barely eight miles through Vacherie to the turnoff for Oak Alley or Baytree Plantations, which are literally next door to each other.

Note: The Oak Alley restaurant closes at 3pm. If you plan to arrive in the area after that time and want to eat dinner, it is necessary to call ahead to either Oak Alley or the Baytree and see if they will cook you dinner. With enough warning, most inn-keepers can deal with any problem. However, should you forget to call ahead, northbounders must stop at the little market in Vacherie (visible from the top of the levee) and buy supplies for use in the inn's well-equipped kitchens. For southbounders, Donaldsonville represents the last chance to visit a real grocery market before the Oak Alley/Baytree stop. Among experienced touring cyclists, it is common practice to pack a few emergency rations..

East bank cycling from Tezcuco to Plaquemine (30 miles via the White Castle ferry)

Cycling along the Mississippi, with only occasional opportunities to cross from one shore to the other, means learning to think far in advance about where you are and where you want to be. If cycling northbound on the east bank from Tezcuco towards the Louisiana towns of Plaquemine, Grosse Tete, New Roads, or St. Francisville, the White Castle ferry represents the first opportunity to cross over to the west bank. The next option, the Plaquemine ferry, is 38 miles from Tezcuco.

Oak Alley/Baytree Plantations to Grosse Tete via Donaldsonville and Plaquemine and the west bank (62 miles)

From the entrance of either Oak Alley or the Baytree, get back up on the levee immediately and turn left (west) for about 16 miles until you bump into another one of those industrial sites blocking the levee trail, forcing a detour onto the paved highway. Fortunately this detour extends for only about one-half mile, and then you can return to the levee for another mile or so to the big bridge. Once at the bridge, you may turn left at the first access road, or go under the bridge and take the next turn to the left. Either way, you should end up southbound on SR 70, with its nice shoulder. Remain on SR 70 for less than half a mile before turning right onto SR 3120 West. This latter road has a very nice paved shoulder for its entire length of four miles. At the end of SR 3210 turn left onto shoulderless SR 18 for two miles into Donaldsonville.

Donaldsonville—a Renaissance hamlet

In the early 19th century, Donaldsonville was the state capital of Louisiana. However, the Civil War and the removal of the capitol to Baton Rouge caused a rather serious decline in Donaldsonville's fortune. Deliverance finally came in the form of John Folse, a chef well-known from Public Television, who formerly had a famous restaurant just a few miles away from "D'ville." When it burned, Folse transformed his Donaldsonville home into a world-class restaurant and B&B, with the modest title of LaFitte's Landing Restaurant and Bittersweet Plantation, located at 404 Clairborne Avenue (225) 473-1232. This relocation has revitalized the sleepy, forgotten hamlet into a gentrified village of restaurants and antique shops. If the $200 per night price at the inn is a bit much, I suggest you at least sample their world-class cuisine. An opportunity such as this will probably not present itself again for a long time.

Northbounders departing Donaldsonville should remain on SR 18 West. Just west of D'ville, turn right onto SR 1 North—a main thoroughfare with a huge paved shoulder—for the next 20 miles or so to Plaquemine and the slightly spooky Gatorland Bike Shop.

About ten miles after departing Donaldsonville you will pass through White Castle, site of another Mississippi River ferry. Southbounders should merely reverse the directions between Oak Alley and Donaldsonville.

Plaquemine's haunted bike shop

(For address/phone, refer to Appendix)

When I first visited the Gatorland Bike Shop in June 1999, I was only looking for local directions, but discovered much more. The proprietors, Rod and Mae Ritterman, have been in the business for years, fixing both bikes and small engines. When I told Mae about my research and how I had been encountering plenty of ghost stories in the various B&Bs along the route, she told me that all sorts of strange things had been happening in their shop, including security systems and lights turning on and off and items moving hither and yon, seemingly on their own.

Mae had been aware of this for years, but hesitated to discuss it with Rod until one day when a bicycle customer came in for some tires. Finding what he wanted, he laid the tires down on the floor and went to pay Rod, who was alone in the store at the time. After completing the transaction, he went to pick up his tires, but ... they were gone! Surprised, he asked Rod about the tires, thinking Rod had moved them. Problem was, Rod had not moved a step away from the cash register, and there was no one else in the shop. Curious, Rod searched for the errant tires. Eventually, he found them—somehow returned to their original spot on the shelf. Naturally, both men were flabbergasted. From that day forward, Mae had no trouble talking to Rod about strange occurrences in the shop.

Plaquemine to Grosse Tete (24 miles)

If northbound from the Gatorland Bike Shop, turn onto SR 75 West for 3.5 miles. Turn right onto Stassi Road North for about 0.9 miles and bear left onto SSR 3055. After 1.5 miles, turn right and cross the Indian Village bridge. Turn left onto SR 77 West and then left again onto the Indian Village Road or Old Highway 7. At the Highway 77 intersection, turn left onto 77 West, cross over the waterway and then head north, still on SR 77, towards Grosse Tete.

At first glance, SR 77 appears to be a pleasantly shaded country road—and it is, for the most part. However, it is also one of the few roads that go through this bayou area, and as such bears a fair amount of traffic. So be cautious, be visible and use a mirror. After 10 miles, turn right onto an unnamed paved road that crosses Bayou Grosse Tete and then immediately turn left onto Sidney Road. This is pleasant, tree-shaded country with little traffic. After four miles you will reach a little jewel in the woods on the right: David's Country Cottages.

Between Grosse Tete and New Roads, Louisiana (30 miles)

From David's Country Cottages continue north on Sidney Road. After one-half mile you will pass under I-10 and then you'll have a pure country road (Highway 411) for fourteen glorious miles to the intersection with US 190 at Livonia. Once across US 190, the road becomes SR 78 and grows busier. Continue straight on 78 for 3.5 miles to Frisco, then turn right onto SSR 979 for 2.5 miles. At the T junction, turn left (north) onto SSR 978 for four miles to rejoin SR 1 with its big, wide paved shoulder.

At the T intersection of SR 978 and 1, turn left onto SR 1 West and continue for 8 miles into New Roads, Louisiana. Note the large body of water on the right, known as False Lake. The lake was actually a section of the Mississippi River until the New Madrid earthquake in the early 1800s changed the river's course.

New Roads, Louisiana

According to local folklore, New Roads (established in 1699) is one of the oldest French settlements in Louisiana. In addition to being directly on the Adventure Cycling Southern Tier route, it is also the last stop before joining Adventure Cycling's Great Rivers Route.

There are two routes from downtown New Roads to the ferry—a direct way (5 miles) and a scenic way (11 miles). The most direct way is SR 1 and SR 10. For the scenic route, go straight through the center of the village onto SR 415 for five miles and bear left onto SR 981 for another 6 miles to the ferry.

New Roads/St. Francisville/Jackson to Natchez, Mississippi (100 miles from St. Francisville)
AC: GR III, 41-43

The three villages of New Roads, St. Francisville, and Jackson, Louisiana constitute a popular bicycle touring destination. Indeed, two major Adventure Cycling routes—the Great Rivers Route and the Southern Tier Route—converge in downtown St. Francisville and run concurrently just to the east of Jackson. So, in addition to local and club riders out for a pleasant weekend ride, one may encounter heavily laden, cross country riders along that stretch.

One reason, of course, is the fact that cycling the area is a delight. On the west bank, New Roads offers great river vistas from tabletop flat roads. On the east bank, there are miles of shaded roads and lightly rolling hills, with little traffic to Jackson and beyond. When you factor in the friendly folks in Jackson, this community stands out as the most bicycle-friendly village encountered on the entire route (though the award for most friendly person goes to, without a doubt, Denny Ward in Marquand, Missouri). For the recommended enhancement to the Great Rivers Route from Jackson to Norwood, Louisiana, refer to page 191.

For info on cycling around Jackson, check with Earl Smith, Director of the Republic of West Florida Historical Museum. An enthusiastic cyclist and member of the Baton Rouge Bicycle Club, Earl has offered the use of museum facilities to touring cyclists. He also has a handle on inexpensive camping in the area. Before you do anything in the Jackson, Louisiana, area connected with bikes, check with Earl. For the museum address and phone number, refer to the Appendix.

Accommodations

Because tourism is one of the main industries in this part of Louisiana, the touring cyclist will have a choice of camping or spending the night in one of several top notch B&Bs, each with a unique ambiance. In St. Francisville, Butler Greenwood's Anne Butler not only runs a magnificent southern plantation that has been in her family for over 200 years, she also has had time to be a successful magazine editor, journalist, and prize- winning childrens' author.

In nearby Jackson, no expense was spared to furnish the opulent Milbank House with world-class antiques. And just a few steps down the street, the Old Centenary Inn has been completely renovated with each accommodation decorated with a different theme. For instance, I stayed in the "Surrey with the Fringe on Top" room, and the bed was—you guessed it—a surrey with the fringe on top.

On the approach to Natchez, Cedar Grove, about seven miles off the route on the Kingston Road, is an elegant antebellum inn with a singletrack trail through the woods for hikers and cyclists. Cedar Grove also provides two high-quality Trek mountain bikes and helmets ready for guest use. On the entire trip from New Orleans to St. Louis, this was the only inn to offer this sort of amenity.

Linden, in Natchez, has such a classic antebellum entrance, you might recognize it as the entrance to Tara in *Gone with the Wind*.

Terrain and services between New Orleans and Natchez

For northbounders, crossing the river from New Roads to St. Francisville means finally encountering some real hills—not just bridge approaches or levees. For those heading south to Baton Rouge or New Orleans, kiss the hills goodbye. North of Jackson, Louisiana, the 90-mile, hilly stretch north of Centreville and along Liberty Road (AC: GR III, 41 & 42) presents a serious challenge.

Along this stretch there are zero—count 'em, *zero*—services between Centreville and Natchez. A garage at the intersection of Tom Crum Road and Highway 33 might be a possible place to refill water bottles. It is absolutely essential for anyone cycling this stretch in either direction to pack extra water and rations. Another possibility is to ride US 61 between the Louisiana line and Natchez. While many have ridden that route and lived to tell about it, this is a major highway, with lots of traffic and several stretches with absolutely no paved shoulder.

Traffic

In general, road traffic on the narrow and shoulderless roads in the immediate New Orleans area is rather brisk and unyielding. This fact makes the levee path even more attractive. From Donaldsonville to Plaquemine, use SR 1 with its wide, paved shoulder and forget the traffic. The suggested route from Plaquemine through Grosse Tete and Livonia to New Roads offers a fair amount of shade and rather low traffic volume.

Once across the river in St. Francisville, northbounders will have joined the classic Great Rivers Route on lovely, tree-shaded back roads with light traffic all the way to Norwood, a mere two miles south of the Mississippi state line. However, between Norwood, Louisiana, and Goulden Road, just two miles north of the state line, the route is on a busy highway with more trucks than cars, requiring heightened caution. The other problematic segment is a nine-mile stretch on Liberty Road between Jeannette Road and US 61, southeast of Natchez. Here one will encounter increased traffic on a narrow, two-lane, undulating road with limited visibility.

Segment Two—Natchez to Nashville (420 miles to the Duck River turnoff & 470 miles into downtown Nashville via Leiper's Creek Road)
AC: GR III, 31-41; II, 24-30

Natchez, Mississippi, and the Trace
With scores of magnificent antebellum homes on tree-shaded streets and plenty of history, Natchez is a delightful city to visit. And because it is the southern terminus of the Trace, it represents a natural break point for those who do not have the time to ride the complete route. The small segment between the temporary southern end of the Natchez Trace and Natchez itself along US 61 used to be something of a white-knuckle ride, but no more. Now you can totally bypass that stretch by departing Natchez to the north along Martin Luther King Boulevard and jogging east via back roads to the Trace. For detailed info on this US 61 bypass refer to page 193.

Cycling the Natchez Trace Parkway (approximately 400 miles)
AC: GR III, 31-41; II, 24-30
With fantastic scenery, no genuine killer hills, very little traffic, absolutely no trucks, a well-maintained road surface, and constant ranger patrols, one could naturally assume that the Natchez Trace Parkway would be one of the most popular cycling experiences in the entire U.S. Until just recently, that was only partially the case. For years, cycling the Trace was more like an endurance event. On one side of the coin, the lack of auto traffic and civilization in general always sounded very appealing. But there was always the other side—lack of infrastructure. Anyone wishing to cycle the Trace had to take along plenty of food and water since it was very difficult to find any sort of supporting infrastructure, such as a market, a water fountain, or overnight accommodations if you did not wish to camp. But that was then and this is now. Today, markets and accommodations are more common, and the situation for touring cyclists has improved significantly. Following is a list of support services to be found along the Natchez Trace Parkway, given in ascending order by mile marker from Natchez.

In case of an emergency on the Natchez Trace Parkway call (800) 300-PARK (7275).

000   B&B: Linden, in Natchez (see page 137). Bike Shop: Natchez Bicycle Center, 334 Main Steet, (601) 446-7794.

008   Camping: Raceway Campground, (601) 445-8279. This campground is located just a few hundred yards south of the Trace. To reach it, it is necessary to cycle about 0.3 miles south on Highway 61 from Emerald Mound Road.

010   Market/Camping/B&B: Country store approximately 1 mile from the Trace on SR 553 East. Follow signs to Natchez State Park, (601) 442-2658. Natchez State Park, about 1 mile beyond the country store to the east of the Trace, is the recommended choice for camping. B&B: Jim's Cabin Rental in Church Hill, about seven miles north on MS 553, is directly opposite the big church.

030   B&B/Restaurant: Rosswood Plantation (see page 153). This is also the location of the Lorman General Store restaurant, situated right next to the Lorman Post Office on US 61. In its current form, the Lorman General Store Restaurant is a surprisingly upscale restaurant. Though you can get an excellent meal, you can no longer buy any camping supplies there.

37, 41 B&B/Camping/Restaurant/Market: In Port Gibson it's the exquisite Oak Square B&B located on US 61 near the middle of the village (see page 151); Canemount Plantation also has a reputation for hosting cycling groups, (800) 423-0684. Camping: Grand Gulf Military Monument Park, (601) 437-5911. Port Gibson has a market and the Old Depot restaurant; for southbounders, the village also represents the last good opportunity to buy dinner supplies before the end of the Trace.

054   Camping: Rocky Springs. Free, but you'll have to compete with RVs.

059   Market: A small country market is located one mile west (left) at the intersection of the Old Port Gibson Road and the Fisher Ferry Road in Reganton. Follow the Utica exit.

Note: For northbounders, this exit also represents the departure point from the Trace for the side trip to Vicksburg via Fisher Ferry Road.

076   B&B: Mamie's Cottage at the Dupree House in Raymond, Mississippi (see page 141). This B&B is immediately adjacent to and directly accessible from the Trace—if you know the landmarks and are able to recognize Dupree Road, which is exactly 2.8 miles south of the SR 467 exit. In early spring and late fall, when the foliage is sparse, the Dupree House is clearly visible from the Trace. Otherwise, during the summer, foliage completely blocks any sight of it. If at all possible, call ahead of your anticipated arrival so that the innkeepers can flag you down or point out helpful landmarks. This will save about 12 miles of backtracking from the exit at MM 79.

079   Market: Several convenience stores and one genuine grocery store located four miles from the Natchez Trace Parkway on SR 467 East in Raymond, Mississippi.

083   **Note to northbounders** on exiting the Natchez Trace Parkway onto the Jackson bypass: There are three ways to get off the Trace for the next couple of miles—one is straightforward and two are rather adventurous.

Method #1 (the straightforward one): At MM 83, simply exit the Trace onto Airport Road/Sam Herring Road. Turn left onto Airport Road and left again onto Raymond-Clinton Road. Continue north to reach the Jackson Bypass.

087   The Natchez Trace Parkway temporarily ends here and picks up again at MM 105. This is also the connection point for the Vicksburg side trip (see page 204). If passing through Jackson, you will encounter a full range of services.

Method #2 for getting off the Trace: Immediately to the right of the last bridge at MM 87 is a well-worn, unpaved path, which you may follow to Frontage Road, below. The intersection of I-20 and Raymond/Clinton Road will be off to your right after about 1.4 miles and represents the southern terminus of the new Jackson Bypass.

Method #3 for getting off the Trace: Continue down the eastbound ramp onto I-20. Just before you reach the interstate itself, on the right you will find a hole in the fence which will allow you to gain access to Frontage Road. Turn left onto Frontage Road East to the truck stop at the intersection of I-20 and Raymond/Clinton Road just over a mile away.

Note to southbounders on regaining access to the Nathez Trace Parkway on the south side of Jackson: Shortly after passing under I-20 on Raymond/Clinton Road, turn right onto Frontage Road West for about 1.4 mile. The very first overpass will be the Natchez Trace Parkway. Just before that overpass, note the worn path off to the left. Follow it up to the Trace. If you are continuing on the Vicksburg side trip, merely continue westbound on Frontage Road and follow the cues for the Vicksburg side trip on page 204.

105   The Natchez Trace Parkway temporarily ends here and is the northern terminus of the Jackson Bypass. If southbound, you will begin encountering shopping malls, restaurants, stores, etc. less than two miles south on Highway 51 (North State Street) as you approach Jackson proper. This situation will continue all the way through Jackson out to the interstate interchange for Raymond/Clinton Road.

B&B/Bike shop: Fairview Inn (see page 127) and Millsaps Buie House (see page 145) 7 and 8 miles off the Trace, respectively. Need a bike shop? Indian Cycle & Fitness, (601) 956-8383, is two miles south of the Mississippi Craft Center and very easy to find. Upon departing the Mississippi Craft Center, turn left onto Highway 51 South. After about 1 mile, bear left onto Ridgewood Road for another 0.8 miles to the next big intersection. Turn right (west) onto County Line. You will find Indian Cycle's new shop after barely 0.2 miles on your right. For those continuing south on the Trace, Indian Cycle is the last shop before Natchez.

MM 87 - 105 is a temporary gap in the Natchez Trace Parkway. This segment is currently known as the Jackson Bypass. As of mid-1999, quite a bit of work had been completed on this, the final segment of the Natchez Trace, and it is conceivable that the entire Parkway will be complete shortly after the beginning of the new millenium. In the meantime, bicycle tourists must continue to use the new and enhanced Bypass or Mid-city route. Refer to page 194.

124   Campground: Ratliff Ferry Campground (Fee), (601) 859-1810. This campground offers showers and a small store.

135   Market/Restaurant: two miles from the Trace on SR 16 West.

146   Market/Restaurant: 0.5 miles from the Trace on SR 429 West.

160   Camping/Market: Koskiusko Visitors' Center (bikes only; free). Believe it or not, there is a rather large Wal-Mart shopping mall at this exit just off the Trace. However, it cannot be seen from the Parkway itself.

180   B&B/Camping/Market/Restaurant: French Camp Academy (FCA); see page 131. In spite of being just a wide spot on the Natchez Trace Parkway, French Camp has it all. The folks who work there, all associated with the FCA, could not be friendlier or more helpful. The FCA dining hall invites visitors to join them for lunch and dinner at $3 per person (summer '99 rate). No reservations required!

193   Camping: Jeff Busby (free, but you'll compete with RVs). *Note:* This is also the location of the *only* gas station/convenience store located directly on the Natchez Trace Parkway.

195   Convenience store: just a few yards east of the Trace on SR 9 East.

204   Convenience store/Market/Motel: Mathiston exit. Convenience store is 0.5 miles from the Trace and a restaurant and motel are just a few yards further on US 82 East. A real supermarket is located 1.5 miles from the Trace on US 82 East/SR 15 South.

220   Market/Restaurant: Convenience store just a few hundred yards west of the Trace on MS 46 West. In Mante, about 1.5 miles west of the Natchez Trace Parkway, you will find two smaller supermarkets.

230   Convenience store: Just a few yards east of the Trace on SR 8 East. If you are looking for a motel, there is one—as well as a B&B—located in Houston, Mississippi, just four miles from the Natchez Trace Parkway on SR 8 West.

234   Camping: Witch Dance (bikes only; free)

243   Camping: Davis Lake, 5 miles west of the Trace; open April to October, (601) 245-3264.

251   Camping/Restaurant/Market: Natchez Trace RV Park, (662) 767-8609, located less than half a mile from the Trace on Pontocola Road/CR 506 East. Convenience store 0.3 miles west of the Trace.

255   Convenience store: 0.7 miles from the Trace on Palmetto Road East.

260   Tupelo: All services including two bike shops. Bicycle Shop & Racquets is located at 1143 West Main Street, (662) 842-7341, about 2 miles from the Trace on SR 6 East, on the right as you bike into town. Use *extreme caution* when cycling SR 6; you will be on it for only a very short time, but the heavy traffic requires intense concentration. Tupelo boasts several hotels and motels, but the real jewel is the Mockingbird Inn B&B on Gloster Street

(see page 147), just one block north of the intersection of MS 6/145. Even though it has been featured in at least half a dozen national and international travel magazines, the Mockingbird remains very reasonable in price. Tupelo's other bike shop—Bicycle Paceline, 2120 West Jackson Street, (601) 844-8660—is less than 300 yards west of the Natchez Trace Parkway on Jackson Street at MM 262. However, since there is no proper exit onto Jackson from the Trace at that point, it will be necessary to make a dirt descent from the Parkway in order to get to the shop. Camping: Tombigbee State Park, (601) 842-7669.

266   Camping: Barnes Crossing, (601) 844-6063, charges a fee; the Tupelo Visitor's Center, (800) 533-0611, is free for bikes.

271   Market/Restaurant: Convenience store 0.5 miles from the Trace on SR 363 West. A small grocery and restaurant is one mile further west in Saltillo.

282   Market/Convenience store: 0.5 miles from the Trace in Kirkville, Mississippi, on SR 371 South.

293   Camping/Market: Whip-Poor-Will Campground at the Whitten Marina, (662) 729-2449, and Piney Grove Campground, (662) 454-3481, are both on Bay Springs Lake, and both charge a fee.

302   B&B/Market: Belmont Hotel (see page 117) is seven miles from the Natchez Trace Parkway on SR 25 East. A small convenience store is 0.5 miles from the Trace on SR 25 West. This market can also be reached via the much safer Tishomingo State Park exit at MM 303 (below). There are several convenience stores along SR 25 between the Trace and Dennis to the east. Regardless of how much you need supplies, avoid cycling on SR 25, which has heavy truck traffic. Refer to the Belmont section for descriptions of back roads through Dennis and into Belmont (eight miles from the Trace).

303   Camping: Tishomingo State Park, (662) 438-6914, has

its own exit off the Natchez Trace Parkway. There is also a market which can be reached via this exit on Highway 25 just opposite the road into Tishomingo. Using the Tishomingo State Park exit at MM 304 will keep you off Highway 25 with its heavy truck traffic. Refer to the Belmont, Mississippi, options (page 117) on how to get to Dennis or Belmont without spending any significant time on SR 25. There are several convenience stores along SR 25 between the Trace and Dennis to the east. Regardless of how much you need supplies, avoid cycling on SR 25.

320   Market/Restaurant: Located in Cherokee, Mississippi, about half a mile from the Trace on US 72 West.

327   Camping: Colbert's Ferry (free for bikes only).

351   Market: Convenience store just off the Trace on SR 13 East.

355   Market: Convenience store located a few hundred yards from the Trace on SR 13 West. A short distance further, less than 0.5 miles from the Trace, there is a supermarket on SR 13 South.

370   Market/Motel/Restaurant: Convenience store just off the Trace on US 64 West. Natchez Trace Motel & Restaurant is located 0.5 miles further west on US 64.

373   Market/Camping: Laurel Hill Wildlife Management Area has a primitive campground 2 miles east of the Trace. At mile 1.9, turn left onto Peter Cave Road. There is a convenience store 2 miles east of the Trace on Laurel Hill Road.

381   Market/Camping: Natchez Trace Parkway Wilderness Preserve, (615) 796 3212, is one mile east of the Trace. This is a members-only campground resort, but it will accept bicycle tourists if space is available.

386   Camping/Market: Meriweather Lewis (free, but you'll be

competing with RVs); convenience store located 2 miles from the Trace on SR 20 East.

391   Market/Restaurant/Motel: SwanView Restaurant/Motel is one mile from the Natchez Trace Parkway on US 412 West. B&B: Ridgetop (see page 185) is located 4 miles from the Trace on US 412 East. It is very bicycle-friendly.

408   Camping/Market/Accommodations: Shady Grove Camping (free) at SR 50 exit. Peden's General Store is located one mile from the Trace on SR 50 West in Shady Grove. This MM is also the convergence point for the Great Rivers Route and Natchez Trace Parkway.

416   Market: Located approximately 1.5 miles from the Parkway on SR 7 East, you'll find Fly's General Store—5661 Leiper's Creek Road, Santa Fe, Tennessee, (615) 682- 2356. B. Wilson Fly's family has been here as long as anyone can remember. In addition to ice cream and snacks, he will also sell you traditional bows, primitive bows, black powder supplies, and provide free advice on how to run the Universe. This is also the recommended point of departure for those continuing northbound into Nashville along Leiper's Creek Road, which runs parallel to the Trace about 1 mile to the east and is much flatter and friendlier than the Trace. It also brings you right by the Namasté Acres B&B (see page 177; also accessible from MM 428 via SR 46 and Leiper's Fork).

428   B&B: Namasté Acres (see page 177) is approximately 2 miles from the Natchez Trace exit via SR 46 East and Leiper's Creek Road South. Hamlet of Leiper's Fork is about one mile to the east and offers a restaurant and market. Camping available at Fiddler's Ridge, (615) 791-8130, one mile from the Trace on SR 46 West.

437   Bike shops in Franklin, nine miles east of the Trace on SR 96 East: Lightning Cycles, 120 4th Avenue South, (615) 794 6050, www.lightning cycles.com; Franklin Bicycle Co., 124 Watson Glen, (615) 790-2702.

Accommodations

In Louisiana and Mississippi, this trip was a series of highs—particularly with accommodations. The Deep South is truly the land of hospitality, and the quality of the various inns I visited certainly supports that reputation. Often, the outward appearance of the inns suggested that I was caught in a time warp—somehow bounced from the dawn of the 21st century back to the middle of the 1800s. Linden in Natchez, Rosswood Plantation in Lorman, and Oak Square *(below)* in Port Gibson immediately come to mind.

Not every inn resembled Tara, the *Gone With The Wind* plantation home that most of us envision when we hear the word "antebellum," but the dedication of the innkeepers, their attention to detail, and the quality of the food that they serve reinforced the idea that Mississippi must have the world's greatest collection of antebellum B&Bs.

Terrain

Throw away the notion that the Natchez Trace is flat. It is in some places, but it can also be quite hilly, particularly as one approaches Nashville. While Trace riders won't have to contend with killer hills, their legs will let them know that they have encountered some legitimate changes in elevation.

Traffic
Except for metropolitan areas like Natchez, Vicksburg, Jackson, Nashville, and Tupelo, traffic was very light everywhere along this stretch. It is easy to become spoiled and let your mind wander.

Jackson, Mississippi, overview
Jackson, Mississippi, used to be a rather tough nut to crack. While Trace riders were reluctant to ride through the middle of the city, the bypass along County Line Road was particularly nasty. Fortunately, the completion of the Highland Colony Parkway has changed that situation dramatically. On page194 you will find two Jackson routes: the new, recommended bypass suggestion, as well as a mid-city route, which leads past the Millsaps Buie B&B and the Fairview Inn. In the meantime, work continues on closing the Natchez Trace Parkway gap between MM 87 & 105.

Side trip to Vicksburg
Anyone cycling the Natchez Trace should seriously consider a side trip to Vicksburg, where vestiges of the infamous Civil War siege abound. In either direction, north- or southbound, it is about half a day off the route, but worth every mile of detour. Refer to "Vicksburg Side Trip," page 204, for details.

Nashville Spur
For both north- and southbound riders, the intersection with TN SR 50 represents a transition onto and off of the Natchez Trace Parkway. This is the point of access into Nashville. Riders bound for St. Louis will leave the security of the Trace and commence a rather hilly stretch all the way through southeastern Missouri. For southbounders, entering the trace is like bicycling into your living room. No trucks, little traffic (except around Tupelo and Jackson, Mississippi), pretty scenery, and delightful B&B and camping accommodations all the way to Natchez and beyond.

Segment Three—Nashville to St. Louis (570 miles or 350 miles via the Marquardt Trail through Prairie du Rocher, Illinois)
AC: GR II, 16-24; I, 9-15 & St. Louis spur.
The natural break point for those going into Nashville rather than continuing on the Great Rivers Route is at MM 408, where the Trace intersects with TN 50. From that intersection it is about a 45-mile ride into downtown Nashville.

Nashville
Nashville—the Capital of Country Music—is a major tourist destination and transportation hub with air, road, river, and rail connections. Although the city center lies about 45 miles from the official Great River Route, it represents a natural breakpoint for the St. Louis and Natchez segments. Using available back roads (Leiper's Creek Road, the Old Natchez Trace, and Percy Warner Park) between Belle Meade and Fly, Tennessee, reduces the exposure to main road traffic to less than ten miles. For detailed instructions on the Nashville Spur refer to page 197.

St. Louis Overview
The beginning or end of this tour—depending on whether you are going north or south, offers even more transportation connections than Nashville.

Terrain
From the SR 50/Natchez Trace Parkway interchange north into Nashville, one will encounter the biggest hills on the Trace. However, the biggest and meanest hills of the entire tour will be encountered on the original Great River Route between Cape Girardeau, Missouri, and St. Louis. Be ready for a series of practice hills between Waverly, Tennessee, and Cave-in-Rock, Illinois.

Traffic
The end of the Trace just south of Nashville will dump you out on Highway 100, a fast two-lane road with little shoulder. For a more bicycle-friendly route into Nashville, exit the Trace at MM 407 (SR 7) and proceed east about two miles before turning left onto Leipers Creek Road North. In the process, you will pass the

Fly General Store. Owner Wilson Fly is a source of advice on just about any topic imaginable. If you need ammunition for your crossbow, advice on your love life, or directions into Nashville, just stop and see Wilson.

For info on the Nashville Spur refer to page 197. Except for St. Louis and Nashville, traffic on this section was generally light. However that does not mean it was easy. The combination of those horrible Missouri hills with rather short-fused dump truck drivers made cycling this segment somewhat exciting.

Accommodations

All of the B&Bs along this segment are simply first class; the innkeepers clearly go out of their way for their guests. Three of the inns had a direct connection with the Civil War: The Riverfront Plantation Inn in Dover, Tennessee, stood right in the middle of the battle for Ft. Donelson; The Nolan House in Waverly, Tennessee, probably hosted Jesse and Frank James, and the Lafayette House in St. Louis was built by Captain James Eads, who constructed the fleet of seven ironclad warships which were so successful in the Civil War river campaigns.

Alternate route between St. Louis and Golconda, Illinois—The Marquardt Trail

If you like hills, then southeast Missouri is the place for you. However, if you would rather forego those hills, then seriously consider the flat alternate route, the "Marquardt Trail," (page 200) which extends from East St. Louis, Illinois, south along the river to its junction with Adventure Cycling's Transcontinental Trail at Ft. Kaskaskia, Illinois, near Chester. You'll have to take your bike on the Metro across the river between downtown St. Louis and East St. Louis.

The inner city segment between the East St. Louis Metro station and neighboring Cahokia is no more than three miles long and can be ridden in less than 20 minutes. South of Cahokia, only the small communities of North Dupo and Dupo stand in the way of being completely out in the countryside and in the river lowlands.

Southbounders will not encounter any real hills until turning onto Adventure Cycling's Trans America Trail near Ft. Kaskaskia. From Ft. Kaskaskia, the eastbound route follows the Trans America Trail (TAT) to Golconda, where it rejoins the original Great Rivers Route to Cave-in-Rock. While it is up and down, the terrain along this latter segment only faintly resembles the Missouri hills.

In addition to a pleasant lack of hills on the Illinois side, both north- and southbound riders will have the opportunity to visit St. Genevieve, Missouri, via the ferry near Modoc, Illinois. Like Vicksburg (but for totally different reasons) St. Genevieve is worth the less-than-five-mile detour and ferry ride. The Illinois side of the river has its share of first-rate accommodations, including La Maison du Rocher B&B in Prairie du Rocher and the Corner George Inn in Maeystown.

A final note of acknowledgment about Marquand, Missouri (AC: GR I, 14). On this trip I encountered a series of "best ofs"—best village, best evening, best breakfast, etc., but for downright best person it has to be Denny Ward of the little hamlet of Marquand, directly on the Great River Route. Upon stopping at the little IGA market to inquire about bicycle touring possibilities, I was immediately turned over to Denny (dward@mines.missouri.org or 573/783 7525), who has taken it upon himself to make Marquand a hospitable stop for bicycle tourists. In a manner similar to June Curry, the renowned "Cookie Lady" of Afton, Virginia, Denny greets touring cyclists and, when possible, lets them camp out in the hamlet's premier tourist attraction, the Pioneer Homestead. There is even talk of turning his home into a B&B.

Limestone Manor, Florence, Alabama

Limestone Manor

901 North Wood Avenue
Florence, AL 35630
Bud & Lois Ellison, Hosts

AC: GR II, 27

RATES:	**Budget - Moderate**
LATITUDE/LONGITUDE:	**N 34 48' 12" W 87 41' 15"**
INTERNET ACCESS:	**From the common area**
WEB SITE:	**www.limestonemanor.com**
E-MAIL:	**Info@limestonemanor.com**
RESERVATION INFO:	**(888) 709-6700**
FAX:	**(256) 765-9920**

After Bud and Lois Ellison became dissatisfied with their corporate existence in the early 1990s, they decided the profession of innkeeping would be much more satisfying. Quite by accident they stumbled onto Florence and were impressed with the city's vision and quality of life. In 1996, they purchased the property that would become the Limestone Manor Bed & Breakfast and opened up for business the very next year.

The Georgian Revival-style home was built in 1908 using Russellville limestone. The first owner was W. C. Ashcraft, a local cotton mill owner, who hosted such luminaries as Thomas Edison, Henry Ford and Humphrey Bogart, each of whom has a suite named after him. All three accommodations are on the second floor; each is very private, bright and cheery.

One unique feature of this inn is the real lion mascot kept by the University of Northern Alabama in an enclosure barely one hundred yards from the Limestone Manor. So far, this is the only B&B on this trip where one can hear a real lion roar. I am assured that the inn has not lost a single overnight guest to a hungry lion, but caution is recommended if strolling about after dark.

Breakfast, served at the guest's convenience, consists of juice, fresh fruit, sausage or bacon, and omelettes seasoned with Lois's own home grown herbs. One of the high points of the breakfast are the whole wheat pancakes that she makes without dairy products. If you choose to go out for dinner, there are numerous high-quality restaurants around the town square, which is a mere five blocks away.

Since opening Limestone Manor to guests, the Ellisons have hosted visitors from over 40 states and five countries. Lois expressed a sentiment familiar to other innkeepers: It is not necessary for them to travel any more, because the world comes to them in the form of their guests

Cycling from Limestone Manor
With sufficient warning, Bud Ellison will shuttle bikes and riders from and to the Trace. There is secure bike storage in the garage. The local terrain, particularly around the University of Northern Alabama campus, is rather hilly. However, the closer to the Trace, the flatter it becomes. The one local loop may be ridden from either Florence inn.

19-mile local tour *(see map on page 64)*
0.0	Begin: intersection of E. Irvine & Wood Ave.
0.1	Right onto N. Seminary St., then bear left onto Wesley St.
0.4	Left onto Circular Rd. which becomes Waterloo Rd. (CR 14)
3.0	Right onto SR 20, then left to continue on CR 14
6.0	Left onto CR 19, which becomes CR 127
10.0	Left onto CR 2
13.0	Left onto SR 20
16.0	Right onto CR 14
18.5	Right onto Wesley St.
18.8	Left onto E. Irvine
19.0	Finish: intersection of E. Irvine & Wood Ave.

Directions to the Limestone Manor
Northbound on the Trace: Shortly after passing over the huge Tennesse River bridge, exit Natchez Trace Parkway at MM 329 onto CR 2 for fifteen miles to the intersection with SR 20. Turn left onto SR 20 North for just over a mile to CR 14. Turn right

onto CR 14 East which becomes Waterloo Road and then Circular Road, which runs through the UNA campus. After about 2 miles turn right onto Wesley Court but get into a low gear since you will have a rather steep hill to climb. After two tenths of a mile, the road bears an easy right onto Seminary. After one block on Seminary, turn left onto East Irvine. The Limestone Manor will be at the next intersection, with the Wood Avenue Inn one long block away north (left) on Wood Avenue. To regain the Natchez Trace Parkway, northbound riders should merely reverse the directions for the southbounders in the following paragraph.

Southbounders should exit the Trace at MM 337 onto SR 20 East. Very shortly after reaching SR 20, turn left onto the back road, SSR 20, which parallels the new highway into Florence. After about ten miles you will rejoin SR 20 South with its nice paved shoulder. After about a mile and a half turn left onto CR 14 East and follow the same northbound directions to the inn. The distance from the Trace to both Florence inns is about 17 miles.

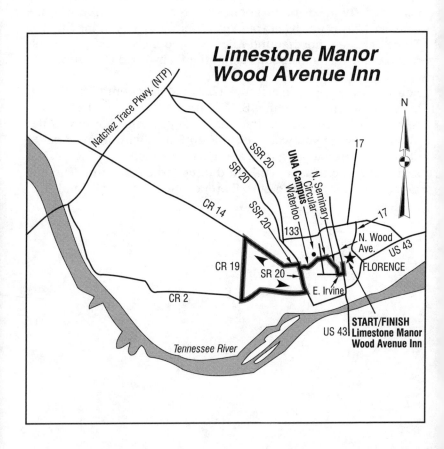

Limestone Manor
Wood Avenue Inn

Natchez Trace Pkwy. (NTP)

SSR 20

SR 20

CR 14

SSR 20

CR 19

SR 20

CR 2

133

UNA Campus
Waterloo

N. Seminary
Circular

17

17

N. Wood
Ave.

US 43

FLORENCE

E. Irvine

N

Tennessee River

START/FINISH
US 43 Limestone Manor
Wood Avenue Inn

Wood Avenue Inn

658 North Wood Avenue   *AC: GR II, 27*
Florence, AL 35630
Gene & Alvern Greeley, Hosts

RATES:	**Budget - Moderate**
LATITUDE/LONGITUDE:	**N 34 48' 27" W 87 40' 40"**
INTERNET ACCESS:	**From hall phone**
WEB SITE:	**www.woodavenueinn.com**
E-MAIL:	**woodaveinn@aol.com**
RESERVATION INFO:	**(256) 766-8441**

The Wood Avenue Inn is a classic Victorian mansion constructed in 1889 in the historic section of Florence immediately adjacent to the University of Northern Alabama. When it was built, the mansion was the first house in Florence to be wired for the electricity which was not yet even available. It also boasted the first indoor commode. During the Civil War, the nearby ROTC building on the UNA campus served as a hospital for both Union and rebel forces. Today, the inn houses five spacious guestrooms.

There are five spacious accommodations with very comfortable beds, and the innkeepers strive to create a romantic atmosphere.

The Greeleys (Horace Greeley was Gene's great, great uncle) purchased the property in 1990 as a private home; the decision to open a B&B came later. They came from California, heading east to Alabama because the cost of retirement is significantly lower. Since deciding to open their home to overnight guests, all their expectations of operating a B&B have been fulfilled. They enjoy interacting with their guests immensely, and they strive to create a romantic atmosphere full of period ambience and privacy.

Breakfast may be the centerpiece of your stay at the Wood Avenue Inn, highlighted by Alvern's excellent sourdough French toast bathed in strawberries. Alvern is flexible with breakfast and, with pre-arrangement, will serve an equally delicious lunch or dinner. In addition, there are several nice restaurants around the nearby town square.

Cycling from Wood Avenue Inn

The local terrain, particularly around the University of Northern Alabama campus, is rather hilly. However, the closer you get to the Natchez Trace, the flatter it becomes. With pre-arrangement, Gene can shuttle bikes to and from the Trace. Secure bicycle storage is available. There is one local loop, which may be ridden from either Florence inn. The nearest bike shop—four miles away—is Bikes Plus Tri-Shop, 3928 Jackson Highway, Sheffield, AL 35660; phone (256) 381-2453.

19-mile local tour

0.0	Begin: intersection of E. Irvine & Wood Ave.
0.1	Right onto N. Seminary St., then bear left onto Wesley St.
0.4	Left onto Circular Rd. which becomes Waterloo Rd. (CR 14)
3.0	Right onto SR 20, then left to continue on CR 14
6.0	Left onto CR 19, which becomes CR 127
10.0	Left onto CR 2
13.0	Left onto SR 20
16.0	Right onto CR 14
18.5	Right onto Wesley St.
18.8	Left onto E. Irvine
19.0	Finish: intersection of E. Irvine & Wood Ave.

Directions to Wood Avenue Inn

The Wood Ave Inn is one block north of the Limestone Manor Bed & Breakfast, on the opposite side of the street, and approximately 17 miles from the Natchez Trace Parkway. Follow directions to the Limestone Manor. At Wood Avenue, merely turn left for one long block and the imposing Victorian manor will reach out and grab you from the right.

Wood Avenue Inn, Florence, Alabama

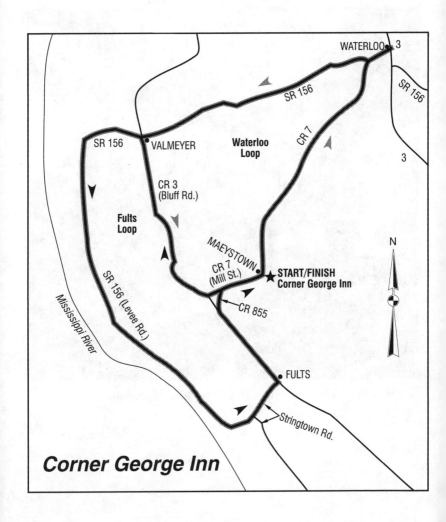

Corner George Inn

Corner George Inn and Bed & Breakfast

Corner of Main & Mill Streets
P.O. Box 103   *AC: N/A*
Maeystown, IL 62256
David and Marcia Braswell, Hosts

RATES:	**Budget - Moderate**
LATITUDE/LONGITUDE:	**N 38 13' 30" W 90 13' 59"**
INTERNET ACCESS:	**From phone in common area**
WEB SITE:	**www.bbonline.com/il/**
	cornergeorge/rooms.html
E-MAIL:	**cornrgeo@htc.net**
RESERVATION INFO:	**(800) 458-6020**
FAX:	**(618) 458-7770**

The village of Maeystown revels in its German heritage and *Gemuetlichkeit*. Founded in 1848, many of the original pioneers came from the Rheinland Palatinate, and the German dialect that one occasionally hears spoken in the area reflects those origins. Of the original settlement, approximately sixty noteworthy structures remain, including founder Jacob Maeys' log cabin, the stone bridge, various barns, outbuildings, Zeitinger's mill and the original stone church where services were held in German until 1943. The entire hamlet has been put on the historic register due to its unusual stone rain gutters.

In 1883, using bricks from his own brickyard, George Hoffmann began construction of the building where the Corner George Inn now stands. When he died suddenly due to a horse-related accident a year later, his wife Sibilia completed the building and operated it as a hotel and saloon until the early 1900s. Over the next several decades it went through various incarnations as the Maeystown General Store, a feed store, and private residence. The origin of the name "Corner George" goes back to 1907, when there were so many George Hoffmanns living in the area that locals needed a system to differentiate between them. Naturally, it was done done with nicknames: There was the *der Lach* (Laughing) Georg, who lived near the bridge in a salt box house, *der Schmitt* (village blacksmith) Georg, *der Dicke* (Fat) Georg, and finally, *der Ecken* (Corner) Georg, who lived on the corner of Main and Mill Streets.

In 1988, David and Marcia Braswell purchased the building and began a restoration. Eighteen months later, they opened their doors as a country inn. Current accommodations include six guestrooms and a cottage, each with a private bath. In addition to sitting rooms and a wine cellar, there is an 800-square-foot ballroom that serves as a commons and dining area on the second floor of the main house, where a full breakfast is served.

The only restaurant in town, Eschy's, is just across the street from The Corner George. It features a lot of tasty German food— even their salad bar is an excellent bargain all by itself. And since this is a genuine German hamlet, you will find the Sweet Shop, which sells sweets and ice cream. Their fudge confections will move even the most jaded palate.

Cycling from the Corner George Inn
There are two interesting local loops. The 26-mile Fultz loop is on table-top flat levee roads, oiled with crushed limestone on top. This could be a bit nasty if one encounters a lot of traffic, but traffic wasn't an issue during my ride. If hill climbing is your thing, try the 29-mile loop that takes you up the bluff to Waterloo. Remember: What goes up also comes down.

26-mile tour along the levee to Fultz
0.0   Start: CR 7/Mill St. Proceed west on CR 7 towards the river.
2.0   Right onto CR 3 (Bluff Rd.)
9.0   Straight onto SR 156.
16.0   Left onto Stringtown Rd. It's easy to miss this turn.
19.0   Left onto CR 3 (Bluff Rd.)
24.0   Right onto CR 855.
26.0   Finish: CR 7/Mill St.

29-mile tour to Waterloo

0.0   Start: CR 7/Mill St. Proceed east on CR 7 towards Waterloo.

9.0   Right onto SR 156. After ½ mile the road bends sharply to the left and becomes Church St. Continue straight on Church St. for three blocks to Mill St. At that point you will be in the center of Waterloo. When done sightseeing, simply retrace the route back to the intersection of CR 7 and SR 156. Continue west on SR 156.

20.0   In Old Valmeyer turn left onto Miller St. which becomes CR 3 (Bluff Rd.)

27.0   Left onto CR 855 (Maeystown Rd.)

29.0   Finish: CR 7/Mill St.

Directions to the Corner George Inn

From the intersection of Bluff Road and CR 7, take CR 7 east for 2 miles into Maeystown. The Corner George Inn will be at the main intersection, to the right in the building marked "General Store."

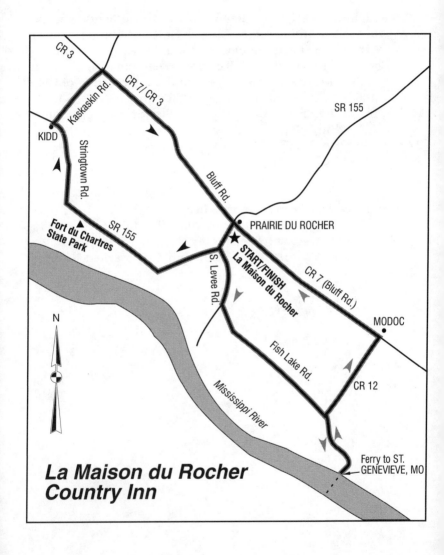

CR 3

CR 7/ CR 3

Kaskaskin Rd.

SR 155

KIDD

Stringtown Rd.

Bluff Rd.

Fort du Chartres
State Park

SR 155

PRAIRIE DU ROCHER

START/FINISH
La Maison du Rocher

CR 7 (Bluff Rd.)

S. Levee Rd.

MODOC

N

Fish Lake Rd.

CR 12

Mississippi River

Ferry to ST.
GENEVIEVE, MO

**La Maison du Rocher
Country Inn**

La Maison du Rocher Country Inn

215 Duclos Street
Prairie du Rocher, IL 62277   *AC: N/A*
Jan Kennedy, Host

RATES:	Budget
LATITUDE/LONGITUDE:	N 38 5' 2" W 90 5' 55"
E-MAIL ADDRESS:	lamaisoncountryinn@htc.net
RESERVATION INFO:	(618) 284-3463

La Maison du Rocher Country Inn was originally erected in 1855 using the local limestone, the quarrying of which remains one of the area's main industries. When Jan Kennedy purchased the property in 1986 with the intent of opening a country inn, she was able to save some of the original beams and mortar and restored the building to its original condition. It now houses four guestrooms and, on the first floor, a full-service restaurant. The innkeeper is also very flexible with breakfast.

According to Jan, an ardent student of local history, Prairie du Rocher was one of the very first French settlements in the entire Illinois territory. It was of such immense strategic value that the French built nearby Fort du Chartres to defend the area. Following Wolfe's victory over Montcalm at Quebec City in 1763, these French possessions passed into British control. However, less than a generation later, Revolutionary War hero George Rogers Clark's tough band of militia and frontiersmen completely surprised the rather isolated British garrisons, conquered the area and almost doubled the area of the United States in one campaign. If you do have the good fortune to spend a couple of extra days cycling about the area, take a moment to stop and ponder the significance of that conquest to the eventual victory of the United Colonies.

Prairie du Rocher maintains a colonial preservation society which works hard to maintain its French heritage. During the Christmas season they put on a special French language musical program which is rather unique in Franco-America.

Cycling from La Maison du Rocher

With genuine historically significant sites, little German and French hamlets scattered about the countryside, and the chance for a ferry ride across the Mississippi to St. Genevieve, Missouri, this is a very pleasant area for day tours. You can pick the flat levee roads or the shaded bluff roads, all rather deserted by cars. Spend a half day at Fort Du Chartres and then cycle over to the ferry, which will take you across the river to St. Genevieve, worth a visit in its own right.

15-mile tour to Fort du Chartres

0.0	Begin at intersection of SR 155 and the Bluff Rd. in Prairie du Rocher. Proceed south on SR 155
4.4	Fort du Chartres. After visiting the fort, continue straight on SR 155, which becomes the Stringtown Rd.
8.0	Right onto Kaskaskia Rd.
10.0	Right onto Bluff Rd. (CR 3)
15.0	Finish at Prairie du Rocher.

15-mile tour to St. Genevieve, Missouri, via the Mississippi River ferry

0.0	Start at intersection of SR 155 and the Bluff Rd. in Prairie du Rocher. Proceed south on SR 155
0.5	Left onto S. Levee Rd.
2.0	Left onto Fish Lake Rd.
6.0	Right onto CR 12
7.5	Arrive St. Genevieve, MO, ferry. For return to Prairie du Rocher, retrace route along CR 12 out to Bluff Rd.
11.0	Straight, then left onto the Bluff Rd.
15.0	Finish in Prairie du Rocher

Directions to La Maison du Rocher

If northbound on CR 7 (Bluff Road), Duclos Street will be on your left near the center of the village. Turn left onto Duclos for about one short block and La Maison du Rocher will be very easy to find on your right. When coming into Prairie du Rocher from the St. Louis area on the Bluff Road, make a right and an easy left to remain on CR 7. Duclos will be the first street on your right after that turn. Turn right onto Duclos and you will easily find the inn about half a block down on your right.

La Maison du Rocher Country Inn, Prairie du Rocher, Illinois

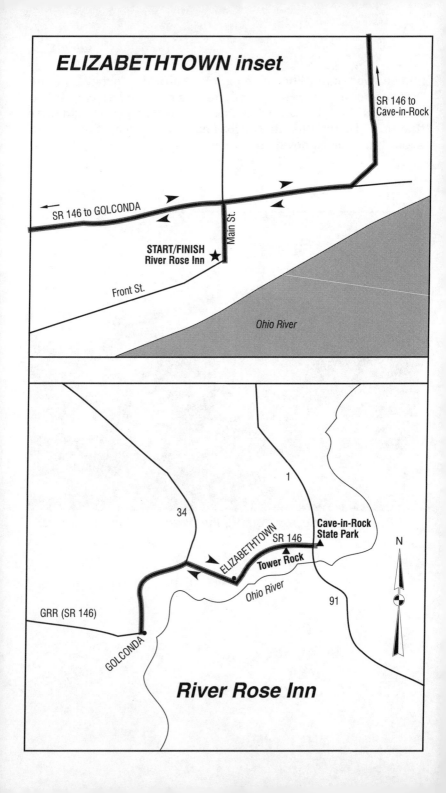

River Rose Inn

1 Main Street
Elizabethtown, IL 62931
Don & Elizabeth Phillips, Hosts

AC: GR II, 18
TAT: X, 117

RATES:	Budget - Moderate
LATITUDE/LONGITUDE:	N 37 26' 51" W 88 18' 23"
INTERNET ACCESS:	From phone in common area
WEB SITE:	www.shawneelink.com/~riverose
E-MAIL:	riverose@shawneelink.com
RESERVATION INFO:	(618) 287-8811
FAX:	(603) 761-8112

The River Rose Inn, an elegant Greek Gothic mansion, was constructed in 1914 in the heart of Elizabethtown, Illinois, with a romantic view of the Ohio River. Four guestrooms are located in the main house, while the honeymoon suite—Magnolia Cottage—is located to the rear of the property. All rooms have a private bath and a tastefully understated décor.

Raised in France and Canada and fluent in French, German, and English, innkeeper Elizabeth Phillips turns out a delicious gourmet breakfast that reflects her European origins. If dining out is on the agenda, the Elizabeth River Restaurant and the Town & Country are just a few steps away in the center of the village.

The village of Elizabethtown played a major role in attracting the innkeepers to the area in 1991. Seemingly pulled straight from a Norman Rockwell painting, the hamlet is located directly astride two national cycling routes: The Great River Route and the Trans America Trail. Even the cross-country cyclists that I met were impressed by Elizabethtown, describing it as "still in the Victorian age" and "pristine." The small town has embraced its position in the cycling universe and the diverse group of visitors that come with it. It is an extremely friendly place to visit, where residents are eager to share the positive aspects of rural life.

Cycling from the River Rose Inn

The 24-mile stretch along SR 146 between Cave-in-Rock and Golconda, Illinois, represents a convergence of the Great River Route and Bikecentennial's original Oregon to Virginia Trans America Trail (TAT). Although the terrain is rather hilly, other cyclists have reported that the traffic along SR 146 was rather light and the drivers polite.

Cross-country riders regularly pass through Elizabethtown and stop at the River Rose Inn, barely 200 yards off the route to the south. The innkeepers are familiar with the needs of the long-distance cyclist, and provide secure bike storage in the garage.

There are no local bike shops. As far as can be determined, the closest bike shop is about 70 miles distant in Carbondale on the Trans American Trail. The next bike shop on the Great River Route is in Cape Girardeau, Missouri.

Directions to the River Rose Inn

At the main intersection of SR 146 and Main Street in Elizabethtown, turn south onto Main Street for 200 yards. The River Rose Inn will be the last house on the right, just before the river.

Wildflowers Farm Bed & Breakfast

348 New Hope Church Road
Calvert City, KY 42029   *AC: GR II, 20*
Carolyn Estes, Host

RATES:	Budget - Moderate
LATITUDE/LONGITUDE:	N36 56' 33" W88 24' 24"
INTERNET ACCESS:	From office phone
WEB SITE:	bbonline.com/ky/wildflowers/
E-MAIL:	crestes@vci.net
RESERVATION INFO:	(270) 527-5449

Nestled in a small, secluded valley amidst a babbling brook and majestic oaks, Wildflowers Farm Bed & Breakfast is convenient to both the Land Between the Lakes and the city of Paducah.

The rambling farmhouse offers 3500 square feet of comfortable living space, plus a large deck in the rear and a covered front porch overlooking the creeks. There are five guestrooms, each with a private bath; two have hot tubs. All rooms are spacious, have a vaulted ceiling and are furnished with all the amenities— perfect for a romantic getaway. The location is far off the beaten path, miles from everywhere, providing a very quiet and serene atmosphere.

Carolyn Estes, the innkeeper, resides on the premises, and is very flexible with breakfast. She's also full of suggestions for local restaurants and other diversions.

Cycling from Wildflowers Farm
Because of the light to medium rollers and the well-maintained and scenic roads, this area has been "discovered" by local riders and touring cyclists. In fact, you'll probably encounter more bicycles than cars on these back roads. Local drivers appear to be yielding and polite. In addition to the one local loop, the excellent network of rather deserted back roads provides ample opportunity to simply explore the countryside in a totally unstructured manner.

There is secure bicycle storage in the enclosed basement. If necessary, the innkeeper will shuttle bikes and riders from and to the Great River Route trail.

The nearest bike shop is 18 miles away in Paducah, Kentucky: Bike World, 848 Joe Clifton Drive, Paducah, 42001; phone (502) 442-0751.

16-mile local tour

0.0	Start: Wildflowers Farm. Proceed West on New Hope Church Rd.
1.5	Right onto SSR 795
3.5	Left onto Dillard Bailey Rd.
4.0	Left onto Sharpe Elva Rd.
4.3	Right onto first paved (unnamed) road
5.0	Right onto Oakland Church Rd.
6.4	Straight across Highway US 68. Road becomes Ecky Rd.
7.3	Right onto CR 795
10.0	Straight across Highway US 68 to remain on CR 795
14.0	Left onto SSR 782
15.5	Left onto SSR 1712
16.0	Left onto New Hope Church Rd.
16.4	Finish: Wildflowers Farm B&B.

Directions to Wildflowers Farm

This out-of-the-way location is 14 miles from the Great River Route trail. Both northbound and southbound riders must turn off the LBL parkway (SSR 453) onto US 62 south and cross the Kentucky Dam. Once across the dam, follow route 641 to the left for about one mile to Lakeview Church Road. Turn right (west) onto Lakeview Church Road which, after about two and a half miles, becomes local route 2595. Continue on 2595 for another two miles to where it T's with SR 95. Turn left onto SR 95 South for about 1.4 miles to US 68. Turn left onto 68 South for three-tenths of a mile and then right onto the Foust Sledd Road. After one-half mile, turn right onto local route 782 West. After two miles turn right onto local route 1712 North for one-half mile to the New Hope Church Road. Turn left onto New Hope Church Road West for about one-half mile to where it drops down into a valley and crosses a small creek. The entrance to the Wildflowers Farm Bed & Breakfast will be at the bottom of that hill on the right.

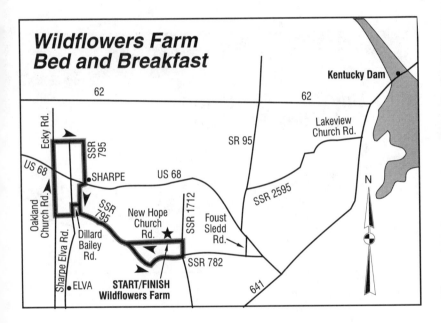

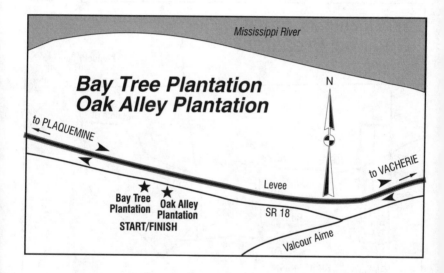

Bay Tree Plantation

3785 Highway 18   *AC: N/A*
Vacherie, LA 70090
Dinah & Rich Laurich, Hosts

RATES:	Budget - Deluxe
LATITUDE/LONGITUDE:	N 30 00' 21" W90 45' 04"
INTERNET ACCESS:	From the common area phone (New Orleans and Baton Rouge are toll calls from this location)
WEB SITE:	www.baytree.net
E-MAIL:	baytree@eatel.net
RESERVATION INFO:	(800) 895-2109
FAX:	(225) 265-7076

With the large flower garden in front, the Bay Tree Plantation looks like it was moved out of a story by the brothers Grimm to its present location. Perhaps it's this fairy tale quality that has given the Bay Tree its substantial Hollywood connection, having hosted famous movie stars as well as Academy Award-winning director Mike Nichols. While filming *Interview with a Vampire* at the neighboring Oak Alley Plantation in 1994, Brad Pitt stayed in the Choppin Room. In 1997, scenes from *Primary Colors* with John Travolta were filmed inside the cottage. Juliette Binoche (Academy Award winner for Best Supporting Actress in *The English Patient*) stayed here while filming a commercial at the nearby Laura Plantation.

Formerly a large sugar cane plantation owned by Edmond Trepagnier—nephew-in-law of Jacques Telesphore Roman, builder of Oak Alley Plantation—the Bay Tree now consists of three separate buildings. The main building is a French Creole Cottage built in the 1850s. Just to the rear of the Cottage is the Rene House, with four elegant rooms with private baths, a common kitchen, dining and sitting rooms. The third structure, a small cottage currently in the process of being renovated, was originally the office of the Oak Alley physician and was later moved onto the

Bay Tree property. When completed, it will offer amenities such as a kitchen, whirlpool bath, and an outdoor Jacuzzi.

Though this bed & breakfast's picturesque appearance and Hollywood connections certainly enhance the ambiance, the real draw is the absolutely delicious classic southern breakfast prepared by Ms. Janetta Gray, the elderly cook. Ms. Gray has the task of providing breakfast for the various Hollywood personalities who occasionally stay at the Inn.

Other than the full-service Oak Alley restaurant, which closes at 3pm, the nearest restaurant is on the far side of Vacherie—about 6 miles away—and closes rather early. Therefore, unless some sort of motorized transportation or adequate bicycle lighting is available, cyclists should buy supplies prior to arrival and count on preparing their own evening meals in the amply equipped kitchen of the Rene House.

Cycling from Bay Tree Plantation
State Route 18, which passes right by the Bay Tree's front door, is a fast, heavily-traveled road, with absolutely no paved shoulder and rather unyielding traffic. Thus the recommended cycling route is on top of the levee—best ridden on a mountain bike, but a road bike with big tires (700 x 32 or larger) should be able to handle the terrain. Bicycles may be securely stowed in the nearby horse barn.

Directions to Bay Tree Plantation
Located immediately adjacent to SR 18, River Road, about 5 miles west of Vacherie, Louisiana, and about 400 feet from the top of the levee path, Bay Tree Plantation is easy to find and very accessible by bicycle.

Butler Greenwood Plantation

8345 U.S. Highway 61
St. Francisville, LA 70775
Anne Butler, Host

AC: GR III, 43
ST VI, 79

RATES:	**Moderate - Deluxe**
LATITUDE/LONGITUDE:	**N30 49' 13" W91 23' 21"**
INTERNET ACCESS:	**From guest room. However, the connection is an extension of the Inn's main line.**
WEB SITE:	**www.butlergreenwood.com**
E-MAIL:	**butlergree@aol.com**
RESERVATION INFO:	**(225) 635-6312**
FAX:	**(225) 635-6370**

Construction of this magnificent home began in 1796 by Samuel Flower, a Quaker physician from Pennsylvania. Now nestled under a canopy of ancient trees covered with Spanish moss, the house includes the finest original Victorian formal parlor in the area. A twelve-piece set of hand-carved rosewood furniture in its original scarlet upholstery, gilded Sèvres vases, a dozen family oil paintings, and windows dressed with their original lambrequins are just a fraction of the many treasures in the main house.

With an M.A. in English from Humboldt State University in California, the Plantation's owner, Anne Butler, is a prolific and accomplished writer, with over ten books to her credit. These include children's stories, travel, crime, cooking, and history. In 1982, she received the Julia B. Collier award and first place in Juvenile Fiction for her first volume of *Little Chase and Big Fat Aunt May*. At the 1983 Deep South Writers Conference her second volume took second prize. In addition to writing fiction, she is also an experienced journalist and editor.

This successful writing career is only half the story. Her roots in this house and the Felicianas go back to the 1790s, when the Spanish Crown gave her great, great, great, great grandfather the land on which Butler Greenwood Plantation now stands. Her children represent the eighth generation of the family to call Butler Greenwood home.

Guests are accommodated in several themed cottages scattered about the property to the rear of the main house. Each cottage has a private bath, and guests prepare their own breakfasts in the completely stocked kitchen. Bikes may be brought into the cabins for secure storage.

The best restaurant in St. Francisville—a favorite of locals and tourists alike—is the Magnolia Café at 5687 Commerce Street, (225) 635-6528, about three miles from the inn. It is only a few steps from the village's only traffic light and main intersection, and is open 10am to 4pm Monday through Friday and until 8pm on Saturday.

Directions to Butler Greenwood

Both north- and southbounders pass through St. Francisville's main intersection of Ferdinand Street, LA 10 & CR 3057, the current (at presstime) starting point for the Great River Route and a convergence point with the Adventure Cycling Southern Tier route. To reach Butler Greenwood from that intersection go north on Commerce Street for about one and a half miles to the Exxon station at US 61. Turn left onto US 61 North for 1.4 miles and Butler Greenwood will be on your left.

For more information on cycling in this area, refer to the chapter on Adventure Cycling's Great River Route, which includes notes on St. Francisville, New Roads, and Jackson, Louisiana.

15.5-mile tour to Audubon State Park

0.0   Begin: Butler Greenwood. Proceed left onto US 61 North.
0.7   Right onto Bains Rd.
5.0   Straight across SR 10 and bear left onto Joe Daniel Rd.
7.5   Right onto SR 965 (**Note:** The entrance to Audubon State Park is barely 0.3 miles to the left on SR 965. This is worth a picnic stop. Upon leaving the park simply turn left to remain on SR 965 South towards St. Francisville.)

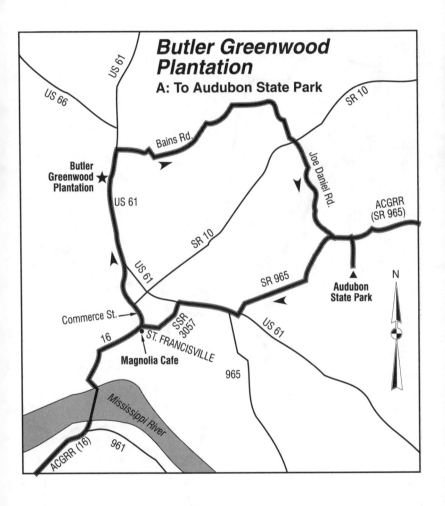

Butler Greenwood Plantation
A: To Audubon State Park

US 61

US 66

Bains Rd.

SR 10

Joe Daniel Rd.

ACGRR (SR 965)

Butler Greenwood Plantation

US 61

SR 10

US 61

SR 965

Audubon State Park

N

Commerce St.

SSR 3057

ST. FRANCISVILLE

Magnolia Cafe

US 61

16

965

Mississippi River

ACGRR (16)

961

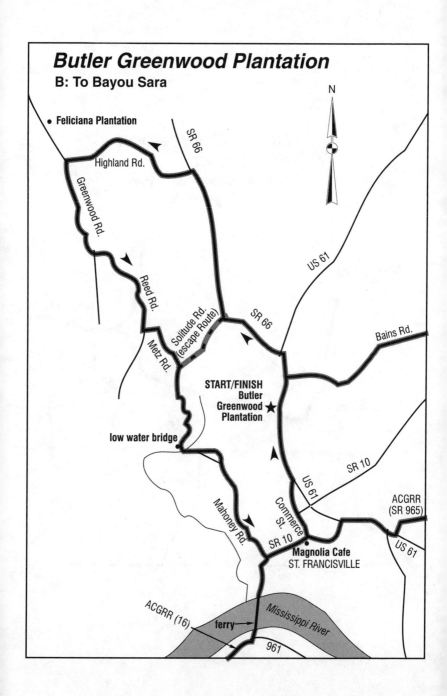

Butler Greenwood Plantation

B: To Bayou Sara

N

• **Feliciana Plantation**

SR 66

Highland Rd.

Greenwood Rd.

Reed Rd.

Metz Rd.

Solitude Rd.
(escape Route)

SR 66

US 61

Bains Rd.

START/FINISH
Butler
Greenwood
Plantation ★

low water bridge

Mahoney Rd.

Commerce St.

US 61

SR 10

ACGRR
(SR 965)

US 61

SR 10

Magnolia Cafe
ST. FRANCISVILLE

ACGRR (16)

ferry →

Mississippi River

961

10.0   Right onto US 61
11.4   Left onto SSR 3057
12.4   Right onto Commerce St.
14.0   Left onto US 61 North
15.5   Finish: Butler Greenwood

24-mile tour to Bayou Sara

0.0   Begin: Butler Greenwood. Proceed left onto US 61
        North.
2.4   Left onto SR 66
7.0   Left onto Highland Rd.
10.0   Left onto Greenwood Rd.
10.7   Left onto Reed Rd.
15.0   Left onto Metz Rd.
16.0   Straight to remain on Metz Rd. At this point Solitude
        Rd. bears off to the left. If high water is blocking the low
        water bridge over Bayou Sara, Solitude Rd. is the work-
        around. At the end of Solitude, bear right onto SR 66
        back to US 61.
18.0   Left onto Mahoney Rd. (eventually becomes Tunica)
20.0   Left onto SR 10
21.0   Left onto Commerce St. at the only traffic light in St.
        Francisville.
22.5   Left onto US 61
24.0   Finish: Butler Greenwood

The Chimes, New Orleans, Louisiana

The Chimes
1146 Constantinople Street   *AC: N/A*
New Orleans, LA 70115
Jill & Charles Abbyad, Hosts

RATES:	**Moderate - Luxury**
LATITUDE/LONGITUDE:	**N 29 55' 27" W 90 05' 50"**
INTERNET ACCESS:	**From the guest room**
WEB SITE:	**www.historiclodging.com**
E-MAIL:	**bedbreak@gnofn.org**
RESERVATION INFO:	**B&B Inc.**
	1021 Moss St., P.O. Box 52257
	New Orleans, LA 70152-2257
	(800) 729-4640 or (504) 488-4640
FAX:	**(504) 488-4639**

Originally built as a one-and-a-half story home in 1876 by a local watchmaker in a quiet, residential neighborhood, The Chimes was purchased in 1991 by Charles and Jill Abbyad with the intent of opening a bed & breakfast. Shortly after purchasing the property from a local sculptor, they began a vast renovation project including the addition of another half story to the house for a total of five guest rooms, each with private entrance and bath. Their semi-enclosed brick courtyard is an oasis of peace and tranquility. They take great pride in serving their guests a gourmet continental breakfast.

Charles, a native of Lebanon and fluent in French, Dutch, Arabic and English, has a degree in hotel/motel management from Penn State. If you are heading out for a meal, check first with Charles, who is the maître d' at one of the upscale French Quarter restaurants; as such, he is quite a resource for the Big Easy's cuisine scene. Jill, a former computer trainer turned full time innkeeper, is a California transplant. She has prepared an extensive folder of area restaurants and attractions for their guests. Both take great pride in their gourmet continental breakfast.

It comes as no surprise that, according to the reservation service, The Chimes has more return business than any other inn in the area. This is due to several measures, not the least of which is the fact that the innkeepers live on the property and go to great lengths to make every visitor feel pampered. For cyclists, a major reason is its location in a serene neighborhood, with quiet back streets that provide solid, bicycle-friendly connections to both the downtown (via the Garden District) and Audubon Park areas. If relying totally on the bicycle for transportation and the weather turns inclement, one can take advantage of either the St. Charles streetcar or Magazine Street bus, both of which are a mere three blocks away.

Writers in particular seem to favor The Chimes: Amy Tan, author of *The Joy Luck Club,* and Bill Moody, Editor of the *Christian Science Monitor,* have been guests here. The close proximity of Tulane and Loyola probably plays a role in attracting the creative writing crowd.

There is ample secure bicycle storage at The Chimes. The nearest bicycle shop is Herwig's Bicycle Store at 5924 Magazine Street.

Directions to The Chimes
For directions to all the New Orleans Inns reviewed in this book, an expanded list of local bicycle shops along with a description of local terrain, road conditions and day tours, refer to "All About New Orleans," beginning on page 23.

Davids' Country Cottages

17985 Sidney Road
P.O. Box 97   _AC: N/A_
Grosse Tete, LA 70740
Jeanie and Richard David, Hosts

RATES:	**Budget**
LATITUDE/LONGITUDE:	**N 30 24' 44" W 91 25' 46"**
INTERNET ACCESS:	**From guest cottage phone.**
WEB SITE:	**www.davidscc.com**
E-MAIL:	**davidscc@eatel.net**
RESERVATION INFO:	**(225) 648-2977**
FAX:	**(225) 648-2187**

Long before becoming innkeepers, Richard & Jeanie David had gained valuable hospitality experience through their catering business. The congenial hosts thought it would be natural to combine that background along with the ability to pamper travelers; the result is David's Country Cottages.

As the name suggests, the inn consists of three shotgun cottages, each over a century old. The cottages are spacious, very private, and—in spite of the presence of I-10 less than a mile away—quite serene. In fact, this is one of the few inns visited on this trip where one could hear the sounds of owls and other night birds. In addition to a television, each cottage is absolutely stuffed with local antiques, which Jeanie has collected over the years. Guests make their own breakfast in the completely equipped kitchen.

Cycling from Davids' Country Cottages

Since the State of Louisiana has decided to route the new Mississippi River Trail (MRT) through New Roads, Grosse Tete, and Plaquemine, the entire area from New Roads south to Plaquemine is rapidly gaining in popularity among both local and long distance cyclists. The flat terrain, shaded back roads, good visibility, low volume traffic, and rather pleasant local drivers all combine to make this area particularly delightful for cycling. A short tour of Bayou Grosse Tete has been included.

Bikes may be stored inside the cottages. And while the seasoned B&B traveler becomes accustomed to tales of hauntings in the usually historic dwellings, this inn offers a unique twist—the closest bicycle shop accessible by bike is the supposedly haunted Gatorland Bicycle Shop in Plaquemine (see page 41).

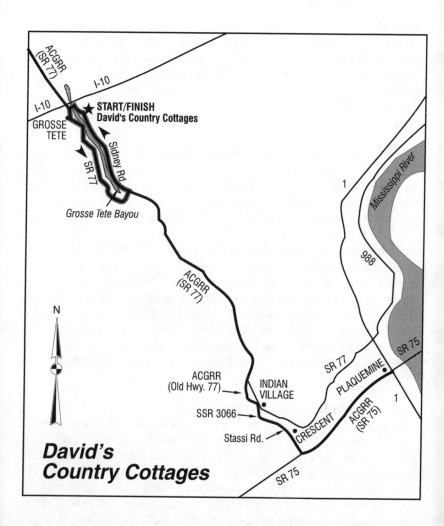

David's
Country Cottages

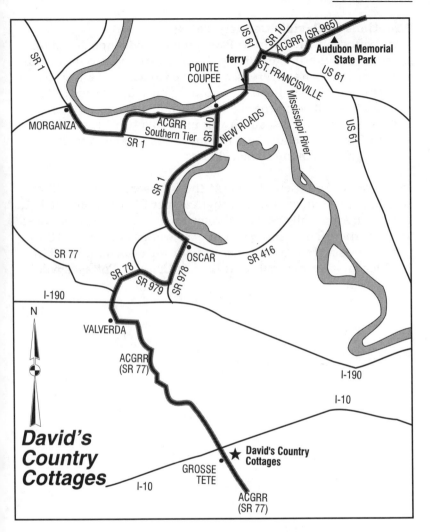

10-mile tour of Bayou Grosse Tete

0.0	Start: Davids' Country Cottages. Proceed north on Sidney Rd.
0.1	Left onto first paved road across the bayou.
0.2	Left onto SR 77
6.2	Left onto unnamed paved road across the bayou and then left onto Sidney Rd.
10.0	Finish: Davids' Country Cottages.

Directions to David's Country Cottages

Northbound on SR 77 from Plaquemine: About ten miles after passing over the Indian Village bridge, turn right onto an unnamed paved road that crosses over the Grosse Tete bayou. Then turn left onto Sidney Road for another four miles. David's Country Cottages will be on the right barely half a mile before passing under I-10. It is no disaster if you miss this turn; just continue on into Grosse Tete and ask for directions. Jeanie and Richard are well known among the local folks.

Southbound from New Roads: At the intersection of SR 78 and SR 190 in Livonia, continue straight across SR 190 onto CR 411, which will eventually become Sidney Road. About fourteen miles south of the SR 190 intersection, you will pass under I-10 exit 139 at Grosse Tete. Continue straight on what is now Sidney Road for another half mile and David's Country Cottages will be on your left.

Lanaux House

547 Esplanade Avenue   *AC: N/A*
New Orleans, LA 70116
Ruth Bodenheimer & Ken Schwartz, Hosts

RATES:	**Moderate - Luxury**
LATITUDE/LONGITUDE:	**N 29 57' 46" W 90 03' 32"**
INTERNET ACCESS:	**From the guest room**
WEB SITE:	**www.historiclodging.com**
E-MAIL:	**bedbreak@gnofn.org**
RESERVATION INFO:	**B&B Inc.**
	1021 Moss St., P.O. Box 52257
	New Orleans, LA 70152-2257
	(800) 729-4640, (504) 488-4640
FAX:	**(504) 488-4639**

This magnificent two-and-a-half-story, Renaissance Revival home was built in 1886 by attorney Charles Edward Johnson, apparently a close friend of Robert E. Lee. As if to underscore the relationship with Lee, owner Ruth Bodenheimer has a letter from Lee to Johnson containing a rosebud from Lee's own garden.

Though the original house had a vast amount of living space—11,000 square feet—it had only two bedrooms (Johnson was a bachelor). After his death in the house in 1896, it passed into the hands of the Lanaux family, remaining a single family home until the 1950s. At that point, it was sold and converted into apartments.

Bodenheimer, the current owner and Director of Publicity for the Mississippi Riverboat Co., purchased the property in 1986. Working with designer Charles Kunz, she immediately began renovations, using some of the original furniture discovered in the attic and original wall coverings. In 1989, to help cover the renovation costs, she began taking in guests. Lanaux House now offers a total of four luxuriously furnished accommodations including the Wieland (the former kitchen) and Johnson suites; the Enchanted Cottage, located in the garden; and the opulent Library suite on the second floor, which comes with a fine view of the French Quarter from a wrought iron balcony.

Bodenheimer feels that the two strong points of the Lanaux House are its location immediately adjacent to the French Quarter and its privacy. Indeed, the renovations were carried out to provide guests as much or as little interaction with other guests as they desire.

She also stated that her greatest inspiration came from a rather unusual source. One evening, she clearly saw the apparition of a man wearing a long coat entering the attic. Having studied the life and times of New Orleans society, she recognized his clothing as a traditional 19th century outfit. Later, after coming into possession of a painting of Charles Johnson, the original owner, she feels that the apparition she had seen had actually been him. In fact, she eventually gave a party on the occasion of his 172nd birthday.

As in the case of many southern homes, the Lanaux House has a Hollywood connection. In 1981, it served as the backdrop for the movie *Cat People* with Nastassja Kinski and Malcolm McDowell.

The Continental breakfast includes chocolate-filled croissants from a local bakery. Guests are also offered complimentary wine and cheese. If you choose to venture out for a meal, the restaurants in the immediate area are too numerous to mention. After all, the French Quarter is just across the boulevard. For a more informal atmosphere, you will find an interesting selection of coffee shops just around the corner along nearby Frenchmen Street in the Marigny district.

Cycling from Lanaux House
Located on Esplanade Avenue, the Lanaux House is near the suggested local loop. Secure bicycle storage is provided in a locked, tree-shaded private courtyard, where you can further protect your bike by securing it to the porch railing.

The nearest full-service bicycle repair facility is just a few steps away:

> Bicycle Michael's
> 622 Frenchmen Street
> New Orleans, LA 70116
> (504) 945-9505
> bikemike@aol.com

Directions to Lanaux House

For directions to all New Orleans inns reviewed in this book, an expanded list of local bicycle shops along with a description of local terrain, road conditions, and day tours, refer to "All About New Orleans," beginning on page 23.

La Maison Marigny, New Orleans, Louisiana

La Maison Marigny

1421 Bourbon Street
New Orleans, LA 70116
John Ramsey & Dewey Donihoo, Hosts

AC: N/A

RATES:	Moderate - Deluxe; minimum stay of two nights. During Mardi Gras there is a five-night minimum.
LATITUDE/LONGITUDE:	N 29 57' 51" W 90 03' 37"
INTERNET ACCESS:	From a phone in common area. Some rooms have an active phone jack—an extension of the main house line—but no phone.
WEB SITE:	www.lamaisonmarigny.com
E-MAIL:	stay@lamaisonmarigny.com
RESERVATION INFO:	B&B Inc.
	1021 Moss St., P.O. Box 52257
	New Orleans LA 70152-2257
	(800) 729-4640
FAX:	(504) 945-5012

La Maison Marigny advertises itself as the only B&B located directly on world-famous Bourbon Street. Though the Inn is officially in the somewhat bohemian Marigny district, the French Quarter is literally just a few steps away on the far side of Esplanade Avenue, and most of the major New Orleans attractions are within easy walking distance. Like the Lanaux House—a mere two blocks away—this inn has one of the best locations in the city.

Originally built as a private home in 1888, La Maison Marigny was converted into a B&B in 1990, with four deluxe accommodations. All have a private bath and one room directly overlooks the quiet, residential end of Bourbon Street. The hosts consider La Maison Marigny to be a concierge B&B; they take an active interest in the needs of their guests. In order help guests enjoy their stay, they often visit other inns to gather new ideas. Their goal is to make visitors feel completely at home.

If you are hungry, you are welcome to rummage around the fridge. The innkeepers serve a delicious breakfast with a preponderance of fresh fruit. In order to help guests choose from the area's many quality restaurants, they have put together a special booklet describing local attractions and restaurants.

For those reluctant to drive a car or ride a bike through the crowded, narrow streets, the Esplanade Avenue bus line and the Riverfront streetcar line are both within a three-block stroll.

Cycling from La Maison Marigny
A description of the local terrain and road conditions are included in section "All About New Orleans," beginning on page 23. Additional local bike shops are listed there as well. The nearest full-service bicycle rental and repair facility is barely 0.4 miles away.

> Bicycle Michael's
> 622 Frenchmen Street
> New Orleans, LA 70116
> (504) 945-9505
> bikemike@aol.com

Secure bicycle storage at this inn involves lashing the bikes to porch pillars behind a high wall and locked front gate.

Directions to La Maison Marigny
Directions to all New Orleans Inns reviewed in this book, an expanded list of bicycle shops, a description of the local terrain and road conditions are included in "All About New Orleans," beginning on page 23.

Milbank Historic House

3045 Bank Street
Jackson, LA 70748
Margurie Collamer, Host

AC: GR III, 43
ST VI, 79

RATES:	**Budget - Moderate**
LATITUDE/LONGITUDE:	**N 30 50' 12" W 91 12' 46"**
WEB SITE:	**www.felicianatourism.org**
RESERVATION INFO:	**(225) 634-5901**

An elegant, antebellum mansion constructed between 1825 and 1835, originally associated with the now defunct Clint and Port Hudson Railroad Company, the Milbank Historic House has experienced various incarnations as a private residence, a hotel, millenary shop, newspaper office, ballroom, and bank. Today it is a bed & breakfast inn with four accommodations: one twin and two double rooms sharing a bath on the second floor, and one downstairs unit with a private bath. The large brick bank vault under the floor of the northeast front room is a holdover from its banking days. During restoration, the inn was furnished with many expensive, museum-quality antiques, creating an atmosphere of absolute opulence.

Innkeeper Margurie Collamer serves a splendid breakfast completely in context with the Milbank's luxurious accommodations. The Bear Corners restaurant, 1674 Charter Street, (225) 634-2844, is conveniently located immediately adjacent to the Milbank House and about 50 yards from the Old Centenary Inn, Jackson's other high-quality bed & breakfast inn.

Cycling from Milbank Historic House

Jackson, Louisiana, is one of the most bicycle-friendly communities I encountered along the entire Great River Route. With scenic, tree-shaded, undulating back roads, low traffic volume, and polite drivers, the area between Jackson and St. Francisville has become quite a mecca for the Baton Rouge Bike Club, as well as visiting cyclists.

This area—also encompassing New Roads—is very easy to reach by bicycle or motor vehicle from either north or south. For those driving into the area, leave your vehicle in either Jackson or St. Francisville and bike to the other village for lunch. On any given weekend in the spring or fall you are more than likely to encounter both local and long-distance riders on the back roads, particularly along the ten-mile stretch between St. Francisville and Jackson, where Adventure Cycling's Great Rivers and Southern Tier routes converge.

There are two local loops each from Jackson and St. Francisville. The Jackson loops begin at the front door of the Republic of West Florida Historical Museum on College Street. The museum director, Earl Smith (earl56@hotmail.com), a cyclist and member of the Baton Rouge Bicycle Club, has offered the use of the museum facilities to touring cyclists. If you're planning to camp, check with Earl. The modification to the Great Rivers Route passes directly in front of the museum on College Street (CR 952). For detailed information on the St. Francisville/Jackson/New Roads modifications to the original Great Rivers Route, consult the St. Francisville/Jackson/New Roads section, page 191.

19-mile Country Loop
0.0   Begin at intersection of SR 10 & 952. Proceed north on SR 952.
10.2 Right onto SR 68.
17.4 Right onto SR 10.
19.4 Finish at intersection of SR 10 & 952.

28-mile tour to Audubon State Park
0.0   Begin at intersection of SR 10 & 952. Proceed West on SR 10.
1.0   Right onto SR 421.
14.0 Left onto Jones Vaughn Creek Rd.
14.5 Right onto Sage Hill Rd.
18.7 Left onto Bains Rd.

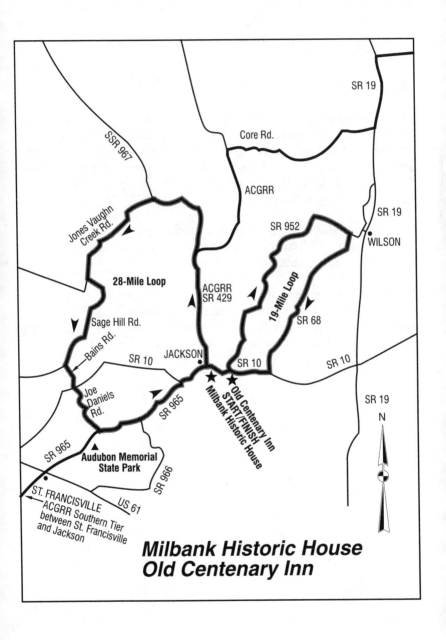

SR 19

Core Rd.

SSR 967

ACGRR

SR 952

SR 19

WILSON

Jones Vaughn
Creek Rd.

28-Mile Loop

19-Mile Loop

ACGRR
SR 429

Sage Hill Rd.

SR 68

Bains Rd.

SR 10

JACKSON

SR 10

SR 10

Joe
Daniels
Rd.

SR 965

Old Centenary Inn
START/FINISH
Milbank Historic House

SR 19

N

SR 965

Audubon Memorial
State Park

SR 966

ST. FRANCISVILLE
ACGRR Southern Tier
between St. Francisville
and Jackson

US 61

Milbank Historic House
Old Centenary Inn

19.6   Easy left onto Joe Daniels Rd.
22.0   Left onto SR 965. *Note:* Audubon State Park will be on the right less than three-tenths of a mile after making this turn.
25.3   Right onto SR 10.
28.0   Finish at intersection of SR 10 & 952

Directions to the Milbank Historic House

When approaching Jackson on SR 10, northbounders should not turn left onto CR 421 but rather continue straight on SR 10 into Jackson. At the Bear Corners restaurant turn right onto Bank Street. The Milbank House will be just around the corner on your right—very easy to find.

If traveling south on the classic Adventure Cycling route, turn left (east) onto SR 10 for less than a mile into Jackson and follow the northbound directions.

If coming into Jackson southbound on the alternative route along CR 952 (College Street), turn right (west) onto SR 10 for one block and left again on Bank Street. The Milbank Historic House will be easy to find on the right.

Oak Alley Plantation, Restaurant & Inn

3645 Highway 18 (Great River Road)
Vacherie, LA 70090   *AC: N/A*
Brandi Quinn, Host

RATES (SUMMER 1999):	Moderate
LATITUDE/LONGITUDE:	N 30 00" 18" W 90 46' 50"
INTERNET ACCESS:	There is one pay phone next to the office
WEB SITE:	www.oakalleyplantation.com
E-MAIL:	oakalleyplantation@att.net
RESERVATION INFO:	(800) 44ALLEY
FAX:	(504) 265-7035

The story of Oak Alley began sometime in the early 1700s, when an obscure French settler built a small house on the site of the present mansion. It was he who planted the twenty-eight live oak trees in two evenly spaced rows, reaching from his house to the Mississippi River. What happened to the Frenchman's small home is not known, but in 1837-1839, a wealthy French sugarcane planter, Jacques Telesphore Roman, built the Greek-revival style mansion for his bride. Nowhere else in the Mississippi Valley is there such a spectacular setting, easily recognizable from the highway or the levee.

Spared the devastations of the Civil War, Oak Alley was sold at auction in 1866. A succession of owners followed until 1925, when Andrew and Josephine Stewart bought the plantation home and its surrounding 1,360 acres to begin what was to be the first of the Great River Road plantation restorations. Mrs. Stewart died in October of 1972, leaving the antebellum mansion and 25 acres to the Oak Alley Foundation, a private, non-profit trust, so that others might continue to enjoy its beauty and dream of its rich past.

Today, there are six accommodations in small, cozy, completely furnished cottages scattered about the property. B&B guests are given free tours of the main mansion. A continental breakfast is served in the plantation's full-service restaurant, which closes at 3pm. If you plan to arrive after 3pm, and you do not want to bike another inch, call ahead using their toll free number to order an evening meal, which will be placed in your cottage. Each guestroom has a fully-equipped kitchen for visitors who bring their own dinner supplies (recommended).

Oak Alley is the venue for several noteworthy special events throughout the year. On the last weekend in March, the Annual Spring Arts and Crafts Festival has become one of the most popular spring shows in the area. Talented artists from all across the country sell, display, and demonstrate their handmade, original creations. Every spring and fall, an outdoor dinner theater is held underneath open-air pavilions. A different play is presented each season by a local production company. On the weekend before Thanksgiving, hundreds of Civil War re-enactors in infantry, artillery, and cavalry units gather for an encampment with daily drills and mock battles. The campsites are open to the public. And finally, on the second Saturday in December is the most spectacular event of the year—the Annual Christmas Bonfire Party. It has become a tradition among the various communities along the river to build huge bonfires on top of the levee to celebrate the Christmas and New Year seasons, and Oak Alley's program is one of the favorites. These occasions are accompanied by special dinners and dances. Reservations are absolutely required for the Bonfire Party.

Oak Alley has a long tradition of unusual events experienced by docents, guests, and staff. On one occasion an entire busload of visitors witnessed a candlestick fly across the room. On other occasions, clocks—which had been inoperative for years—suddenly began ticking. The anecdotes about mysterious events are simply too numerous to mention. During the tour of the mansion (free to overnight guests), the docents will regale one and all with tales of strange sightings and unusual occurrences.

Cycling from Oak Alley Plantation

The closest bike shop is The Bicycle Connection in Gonzales, about 26 miles away.

> The Bicycle Connection
> 108 East Ascension Street
> Gonzales, LA 70737
> (225) 647-9352

However, it is almost impossible to get across the river on a bicycle at this point. For northbounders, the next accessible bike shop will be the Gatorland Bicycle Shop in Plaquemine, 47 miles away. If southbound, the next shops are in New Orleans.

Directions to Oak Alley Plantation

If northbound, Oak Alley Plantation is very easy to find about four miles west of Vacherie immediately adjacent to SR 18. If cycling southbound on top of the levee, Oak Alley is 16 miles south of the Sunshine Bridge (SR 70). Just look for the splendid mansion framed in rows of ancient oak trees on the west side of the highway.

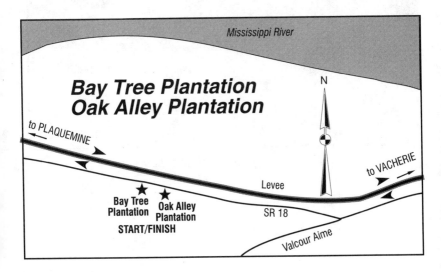

Old Centenary Inn, Jackson, Louisiana

Old Centenary Inn

1740 Charter Street
P.O. Box 1000
Jackson, LA 70748
Ms. Jimmie Best, Host

AC: GR III, 43
ST VI, 79

RATES:	Moderate - Deluxe
LATITUDE/LONGITUDE:	N 30 50' 13" W 91 12' 52"
INTERNET ACCESS:	From guest room
WEB SITE:	www.felicianatourism.org
RESERVATION INFO:	(225) 634-5050
FAX:	(225) 634-5151

From the time it was built in 1935, the Old Centenary Inn has been associated with the hospitality industry. While its spacious facilities were designed to accommodate large weddings and receptions, the private New Orleans-style patio and the private balconies on the second floor offer the combination of privacy and coziness that you expect from a small inn. Each of the eight accommodations has been uniquely decorated with a specific theme. For example, the bed in the "Surry With a Fringe On Top" room was modeled after—yes—a covered surrey. As with its sister inn around the corner, the Historic Milbank House, no expense was spared for the furnishings.

Innkeeper Jimmie Best grows her own mint, and provides a complimentary mint julep to guests upon check-in. The hospitality continues in the morning, with a full breakfast served in the large dining room. If you plan to dine out, The Bear Corners restaurant is conveniently located between the Milbank House and the Old Centenary Inn on the southwest corner of the intersection of Charter and Bank Streets; call (225) 634-2844.

Cycling from the Old Centenary Inn

While both inns offer a warm and friendly ambience, the real attraction is the village of Jackson itself, which is very bicycle-friendly. If you need information on cycling in the area, Earl Smith, the curator of the West Feliciana Museum in Jackson and an active member of the Baton Rouge cycling club, is the man to ask. He has opened the museum facilities to cyclists, and has information on inexpensive camping in the area. Drop him an e-mail at earl56@hotmail.com before coming to the area. Several area loops, which pass by the museum and are regularly used by the Baton Rouge club, have been included in this book.

Except for sometimes busy Highway 10 (which the local law enforcement authorities are said to monitor rather closely), the surrounding roads are lightly rolling, often tree-shaded, in good repair, and the drivers are polite. On any given weekend, one is apt to see many cyclists throughout the area thanks to its proximity to St. Francisville, barely 10 miles away, itself a major cycling destination. Also, the back road connection between St. Francisville and Jackson represents a common location for both the Adventure Cycling's Great Rivers Route and Southern Tier Route. It is not at all unusual to encounter heavily-laden long distance riders along this stretch.

Note: *Refer to page 105 to view the map for the following loops.*

19-mile Country Loop
0.0	Begin at intersection of SR 10 & 952. Proceed north on SR 952.
10.2	Right onto SR 68.
17.4	Right onto SR 10.
19.4	Finish at intersection of SR 10 & 952.

28-mile tour to Audubon State Park
0.0	Begin at intersection of SR 10 & 952. Proceed West on SR 10.
1.0	Right onto SR 421.
14.0	Left onto Jones Vaughn Creek Rd.
14.5	Right onto Sage Hill Rd.
18.7	Left onto Bains Rd.
19.6	Easy left onto Joe Daniels Rd.
22.0	Left onto SR 965. *Note:* Audubon State Park will be on the right less than three-tenths of a mile after making this turn.

25.3   Right onto SR 10.

28.0   Finish at intersection of SR 10 & 952.

Directions to Old Centenary Inn

If northbound on SR 10: At the intersection of CR 421 & SR 10 just west of Jackson, continue straight on 10 less than one mile into Jackson. The Old Centenary Inn will be on the right (very easy to find) at the eastern end of the village.

If southbound on CR 421: At the intersection of 421 & SR 10, turn left (east) onto SR 10 less than one mile into Jackson. The Old Centenary Inn will be on the right (very easy to find) at the eastern end of the village.

If coming into Jackson on the alternative route along CR 952 (College Street): Turn right (west) onto SR 10 and the Old Centenary Inn will be on the left.

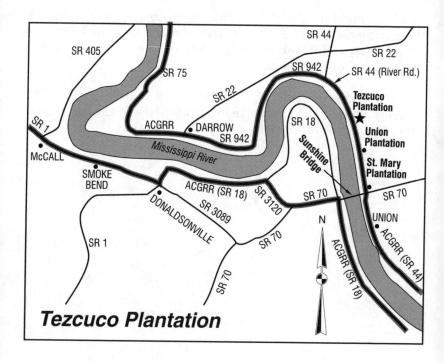

SR 405

SR 44

SR 22

SR 75

SR 942

SR 44 (River Rd.)

SR 22

Tezcuco
Plantation

SR 1

ACGRR   • DARROW
SR 942

SR 18

★   Union
Plantation

McCALL

Mississippi River

Sunshine
Bridge

St. Mary
Plantation

SMOKE
BEND

ACGRR (SR 18)   SR 3120   SR 70

SR 70

DONALDSONVILLE

SR 3089

N

UNION

ACGRR (SR 44)

SR 1

SR 70

ACGRR (SR 18)

SR 70

Tezcuco Plantation

Tezcuco Plantation

3138 Highway 44   *AC: N/A*
Darrow, LA 70725
Annette Harland, Host

RATES:	**Budget - Deluxe**
LATITUDE/LONGITUDE:	**N 30 6' 8" W 90 54' 28"**
WEB SITE:	**www.tezcuco.com**
RESERVATION INFO:	**(877) 567-3334 or (225) 562-3929**
FAX:	**(225) 562-3923**

Along with Oak Alley and Nottoway Plantations, Tezcuco Plantation is known as one of the three *grandes dames* of the Mississippi. Built in 1855 by Benjamin F. Turead using home-made brick and Louisiana cypress, Tezcuco's main house is a Greek Revival raised cottage. The plantation offers a total of 26 accommodations: 23 in the small cottages and three guestrooms in the main mansion.

Tezcuco's most surprising and unusual feature is the small Civil War museum, wherein I discovered the remains of a Confederate semi-submersible boat. Technically, it was not a submarine but rather a hand-powered watercraft designed so that only a small area of the control bridge was exposed above the waterline. Evidently this particular boat was never used in combat and remains in a remarkable state of preservation.

The Cabin Restaurant, located on the property, serves excellent lunches and dinners. Though it does not serve breakfast to the general public, the restaurant staff delivers a full breakfast to the rooms of B&B guests. Every employee of the plantation, from the night crew to the restaurant staff, was extremely friendly and helpful.

Cycling from Tezcuco Plantation
Tezcuco lies directly adjacent to River Road on the east bank of the Mississippi River, about 200 feet from the levee trail and about one mile west of the Sunshine bridge on Highway 18.

The crushed limestone path atop the levee is manageable on a road bike with wide tires (700 x 32 and up). The surface of Highway 44 is in average to good condition. What little highway traffic there is during the day is mostly semi-trucks servicing the nearby industrial sites. Shift changes at the nearby plants also bring a rather brisk amount of traffic. It is suggested that cyclists remain on top of the levee and come down onto the paved highway only when necessary.

The bicycle shop nearest to Tezcuco is about ten miles away via Highway 44:

> The Bicycle Connection
> 108 East Ascension Street
> Gonzales, LA 70737
> (225) 647-9352

For secure stowage, bikes may be brought into the guestrooms. Depending on the distances involved and available staff, bikes and/or gear may be shuttled to another location for a fee.

Directions to Tezcuco Plantation

Riders headed into Baton Rouge should remain on this—the east— side of the river and ride the levee trail as far as possible. When you come off the levee, you will be on River Road, which will bring you through the LSU campus and into Baton Rouge proper. If headed northbound to New Roads/St. Francisville and you wish to avoid the Baton Rouge hassle, cross the river via either the White Castle or Plaquemine ferries. West bank riders southbound into New Orleans should cross the river at either the Veterans Memorial Bridge just east of Vacherie or take the Edgard ferry. **Note:** Except for the ferries and the Veterans Memorial Bridge, there is no bicycle-friendly route across the Mississippi River in Louisiana north of New Orleans.

Belmont Hotel

121 Main Street
Belmont, MS 38827
Ron & Pat Deaton, Hosts

AC: GR II, 28

RATES:	**Budget**
LATITUDE/LONGITUDE:	**N 34 30' 35" W 88 12' 29"**
INTERNET ACCESS:	**Phone jack in dining room**
RESERVATION INFO:	**(888) 826-6023 or (662) 454-7948**

Several years ago, with the demise of the local apparel industry, Belmont natives Ron and Pat Deaton decided to buy the aging Belmont Hotel, built in 1924, and operate it as a bed & breakfast hotel. In 1995—a mere six months after closing the deal—they opened up their doors to overnight guests with 15 accommodations. The only hotel accommodations in the area, the Belmont has been a success ever since.

Don't be misled by the weathered Belmont Hotel sign on the outside. Once inside, the difference is like night and day, with a renovated interior, highly polished pine floors, and a formal dining room that doubles as the breakfast room for guests. Pat even copied Nancy Reagan's White House drapes. In addition to replacing the weathered sign over the front door, she intends to spruce up the outside with plants and wrought iron chairs and benches.

Since Pat works full time at the local hospital, the day-to-day operation of the hotel has become Ron's responsibility. He has a small trailer to shuttle bikes around, and has been known to occasionally loan out his car to guests so they can get dinner (the Sparks Drive-in, about one mile away, is a full-service restaurant—don't be misled by the name). Every morning, Ron serves an enhanced continental breakfast with cereals, fruit, and juices.

Both Ron and Pat feel that the hotel is home to some sort of benevolent though prankish entity, which likes to turn TVs and water faucets on and off. On numerous occasions they have distinctly heard voices when no one else was there. In one instance, there was such a loud crash that several overnight guests came out to see what had happened. But they could find nothing amiss.

The innkeepers speculate that their invisible guest might be the former owner, a banker who purchased the property in 1940. He operated the hotel until his death in 1965. His wife and her sister stored all of his possessions in Room 12 and continued to run the hotel until 1995, when the Deatons purchased the property.

Belmont, Mississippi, with a population of about 2000, is blessed with not only the Belmont Hotel, but three campgrounds within a radius of 15 miles from the center of the village. Tishomingo State Park, almost due north of Belmont as the crow flies, can be reached directly from the Trace via its own exit at MM 304. Just about 11 miles further to the south, two campgrounds can be reached via the Natchez Trace exit at MM 293. Upon exiting the Trace, turn left (north) and bear left on CR 1 for one mile to MS 4. At that intersection turning left (west), crossing the bridge and then right into the marina will bring you to the Bay Springs Marina & Campground, P.O. Box 48, CR 3495, New Site, Mississippi, 38859; (622) 728-2449. Turning right onto CR 1 East will bring you to the Piney Grove Campground; (662) 728-1134.

Cycling from the Belmont Hotel

The local terrain is mostly light to medium rollers, with no severe hills observed. There is secure bicycle storage in the ice room. The inn is an easy eight-mile ride from the Natchez Trace and the Adventure Cycling Great River Route. The nearest bike shop is in Tupelo, 45 miles away.

Directions to the Belmont Hotel

Both north- and southbound riders must exit the Natchez Trace Parkway at MM 302—marked Belmont & MS 25. You will cross and re-cross SR 25 for the next 8 miles into Belmont. Coming off the Trace, make a sharp right turn onto a small, unnamed, tree-shaded road for one mile until it joins SR 25. Turn right onto SR 25 East and then immediately make another right onto the first paved—but again unnamed—road. After less than one quarter of a mile, bear left onto the first paved, unnamed road which again parallels

SR 25. After one mile this road will cross SR 25. Continue straight across SR 25. After about one quarter mile, follow the road to the right and it will rejoin SR 25 after about half a mile. Go left onto 25 East; ignore SR 4 but take the very first paved road to the right which is just a few yards past SR 4. Continue on this unnamed road until it re-crosses SR 25 after less than half a mile. Here you must cycle about four tenths of a mile on busy SR 25 before turning left and crossing the train tracks onto Old Highway 25. It will eventually become the Old Stone Road and after about two and a half miles of following the tracks will bring you right onto Front St. in Belmont. Turn left onto Front Street; the Belmont Hotel will be on the right after two short blocks.

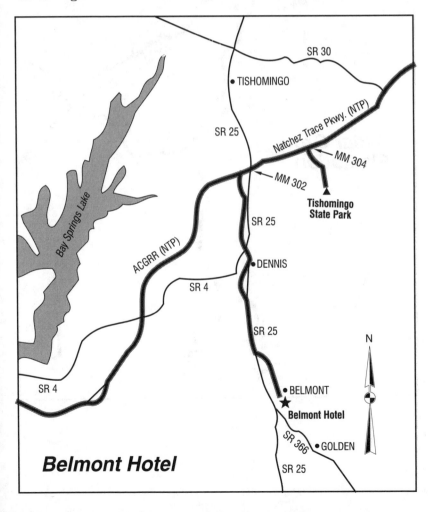

Belmont Hotel

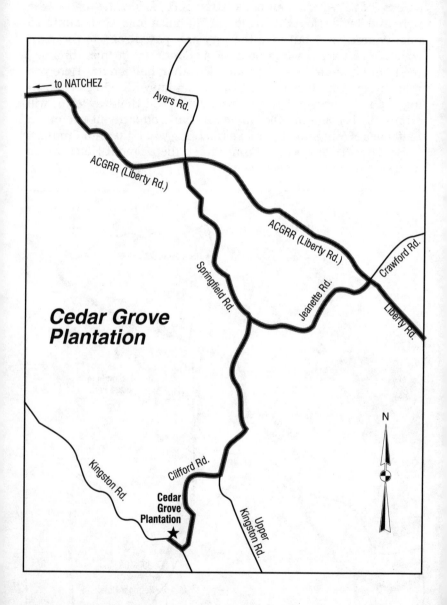

Cedar Grove Plantation

617 Kingston Road
Natchez, MS 39120
Layne Taylor, Host

AC: GR III, 41

RATES:	**Moderate - Deluxe**
LATITUDE/LONGITUDE:	**N 31 33' 32" W 91 29' 26"**
INTERNET ACCESS:	**From the kitchen phone, an extension of the main phone line.**
WEB SITE:	**www.cedargroveplantation.com**
E-MAIL:	**Cedargroveplantation@bkbank.com**
RESERVATION INFO:	**(877) 508-6800 or (601) 445-0585**
FAX:	**(601) 446-5150**

Cedar Grove, once the center of a 900-acre cotton plantation, is located in an area of scenic, canopied country roads about ten miles southeast of Natchez. The brick, one-and-a-half story Greek Revival main house, constructed in 1830, is a perfect base for short day rides. The original occupant, Absolom Sharp of New Jersey, decided to forego the usual front gallery for a rear porch overlooking the rose garden and one of the five ponds scattered throughout the current 150 acres. A den with TV and a library full of books greatly enhance the coziness and ambience. In addition to the five accommodations in the main house, there are two very private guestrooms in the carriage house overlooking the pool. All guests are served a full plantation breakfast in the breakfast nook.

Due to its somewhat remote location and typically high occupancy rate, the innkeeper cautions against arriving without a reservation. Dinner reservations are also a must.

This is the only inn profiled in this book which has resources specifically dedicated to cycling and hiking. In addition to maintaining two good-quality mountain bikes and helmets for guest use, the staff has created a scenic, unpaved hiking/cycling path that winds throughout the property.

Directions to Cedar Grove Plantation

If northbound on Liberty Road, turn left onto Jeannette Road for three miles. Bear left again onto Upper Kingston Road for three miles. Turn right onto Clifford Road for 2.3 miles to where it ends at a T. Turn right onto Kingston Road and the entrance to Cedar Grove will be on the right. If continuing northbound towards Natchez, simply turn right onto Kingston Road for six miles to Highway 61. Turn right onto Highway 61 North and ride along a wide paved shoulder for four miles into Natchez.

If southbound out of Natchez you will be able to avoid a significant stretch of Liberty Road simply by continuing south to Kingston Road. The following directions are based on the intersection of US 61 and Liberty Road in Natchez:

From Natchez continue south on US 61 for four miles. Turn left onto Kingston Road for six miles and Cedar Grove Plantation will pop up on the left. If continuing southbound on the Adventure Cycling route, simply reverse the northbound instructions back to Liberty Road and continue south towards St. Francisville.

Cedar Grove Plantation, Natchez, Mississippi

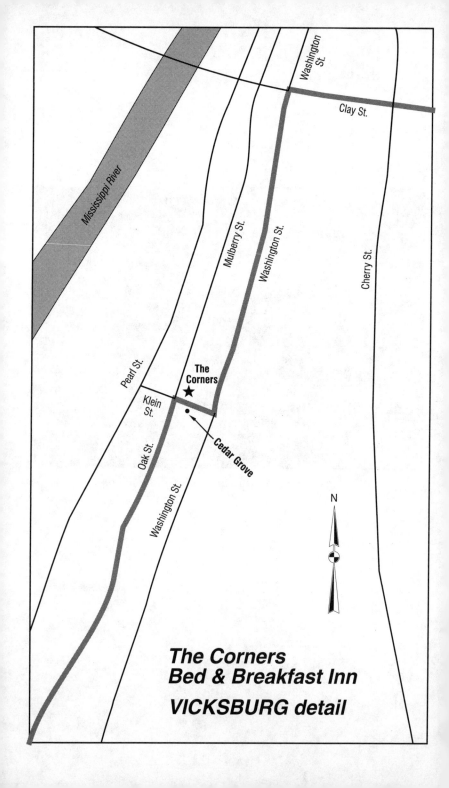

Mississippi River

Washington St.

Clay St.

Mulberry St.

Washington St.

Cherry St.

Pearl St.

The Corners
★

Klein St.

Cedar Grove

Oak St.

Washington St.

N

The Corners
Bed & Breakfast Inn

VICKSBURG detail

The Corners Bed & Breakfast Inn

601 Klein Street
Vicksburg, MS 39180   *AC: N/A*
Bettye, Cliff, & Kilby Whitney, Hosts

RATES:	**Budget - Moderate**
LATITUDE/LONGITUDE:	**N32 20' 59" W 90 53' 29"**
INTERNET ACCESS:	**From guestroom phone.**
WEB SITE:	**www.thecorners.com**
E-MAIL:	**Info@cornersb.magnolia.net**
RESERVATION INFO:	**(800) 444-7421**

Built in 1873 in an eclectic architectural style, The Corners Bed & Breakfast Inn resembles a southern Louisiana raised cottage with large windows for admitting lots of ambient light. There are a total of 15 accommodations in the main building, a cottage across the street, and a new, contemporary addition with a fine view of the Mississippi River. All rooms are completely furnished with TV, telephones, and a private bath. Some have a canopy bed, fireplace, or Jacuzzi.

While the furnishings are lavish, The Corners avoids the museum-like atmosphere that befalls some inns that are stuffed with untouchable antiques. Here, everything is to be used. The innkeepers are quick to point out that the guests are welcome throughout their home. If the opportunity presents itself, try to coax innkeeper Bettye Whitney into spinning some of her yarns about The Corners. On the occasion of my visit, she had everyone's complete and undivided attention—she's a brilliant raconteur.

The inn is perched on the side of one of the many steep hills throughout Vicksburg. Those hills and the commanding view of the river below made Vicksburg a strategic location during the Civil War, and were the reason for the famous Civil War siege that devastated the community. Ironically, the residents of Vicksburg had voted *not* to secede from the Union. As you would expect, statues and relics of the battles are everywhere. Though only about 50 miles off the Great Rivers Route, Vicksburg is clearly worth the detour.

Directions to The Corners
For directions to The Corners, refer to the cues to the Vicksburg Side Trip on page 204.

The Corners Bed & Breakfast Inn, Vicksburg, Mississippi

Fairview Inn

734 Fairview Street   *AC: GR III, 37*
Jackson, MS 39202
Carol and Bill Simmons, Hosts

RATES:	**Moderate - Deluxe**
LATITUDE/LONGITUDE:	**N 32 19' 14" W 90 10' 37"**
INTERNET ACCESS:	**From the guest room**
WEB SITE:	**www.fairviewinn.com**
E-MAIL:	**fairview@fairviewinn.com**
RESERVATION INFO:	**(888) 948-1908**

The Fairview Inn was constructed in 1908 for lumber magnate Cyrus Carl Warren in the Colonial Revival style. The architect, Robert Closson Spencer from Chicago, was a close associate of Frank Lloyd Wright, and Fairview remains the only Colonial house Closson ever designed. The conversion into an inn resulted in a few minor modifications to the original layout in order to accommodate the eight luxurious accommodations.

Carol and Bill Simmons acquired the property from Bill's family in 1972 but waited until 1993 to reincarnate it as a B&B. Even though the inn is very large and one of the most elegant on this tour, the physical layout is unique, with the main house and the carriage house connected via a large covered garden room. In this manner, several of the eight rooms and suites were tucked away in remote corners of the inn, assuring privacy where desired, all the while giving an air of adventure and discovery. In fact, several of the staff mentioned that it took several weeks just to find out where everything is located.

With a Masters in dietetics, Carol oversees the production of all the food for weddings and receptions in their large, commercial grade kitchen. She is currently developing dinner and picnic menus for the overnight B&B guests. Off-site dining options include Kiefer's, a mere four blocks away, which takes only cash—no exceptions. Fenian's Irish restaurant is also just a couple of blocks away.

Besides interruptions to serve with the Royal Engineers and OSS in WW II, Innkeeper Bob Simmons has actually called the Fairview Inn home since the 1930s. As a young man, he arrived in Europe in early 1939 to study French and was in Tours during the fall of France but escaped through Italy. After completing a tour with the Royal Engineers from 1940-41, he returned to the United States and eventually ended up working for the OSS on a project to hunt down stolen Nazi treasure. Bob has the appearance of a southern Colonel and is very interesting to chat with. Carol and Bob got into the B&B business because the property was so expensive to keep up. They enjoy the business immensely and are active in the PAII (Professional Association of Innkeepers International).

Cycling from the Fairview Inn
Since Jackson is the state capital, there is quite a bit of traffic on the main thoroughfares. However, the residential streets, though somewhat hilly, appear to be rather devoid of cars. On occasion, the innkeeper has shuttled bicycles from and to the Trace.

Local area bike shops include:

> The Bike Rack
> 2282 Lakeland Dr
> Flowood, MS 39208
> (601) 936-2100
>
> Indian Cycle
> P.O. Box 1287
> 125 Dyess Rd
> Ridgeland, MS 39157
> (601) 956-8383
> (800) 898-0019
> (601) 956-6230

Directions to the Fairview Inn

The Fairview's location, just off North State Street, in the rather upscale Bellhaven Historic District and a close commute to the state capitol, is far enough away to avoid any traffic noise. Similar to the nearby Millsaps Buie House, bicycle access from the Trace's northern terminus in Ridgeland could not be easier. For detailed instructions on how to find both the Fairview Inn and the Millsaps Buie House refer to page 196.

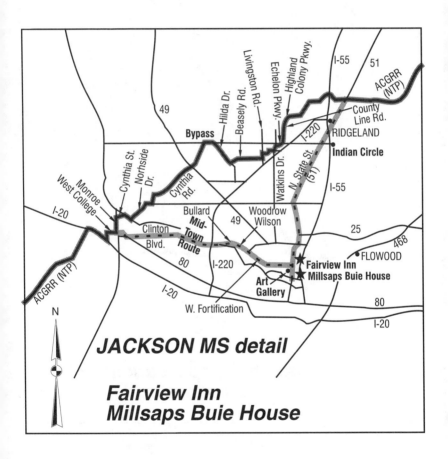

JACKSON MS detail

Fairview Inn
Millsaps Buie House

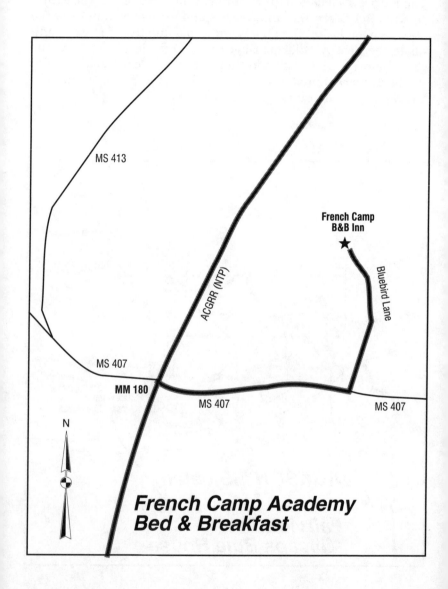

MS 413

French Camp
B&B Inn
★

ACGRR (NTP)

Bluebird Lane

MS 407

MM 180

MS 407

MS 407

N

French Camp Academy
Bed & Breakfast

French Camp Academy Bed & Breakfast

1 Bluebird Lane
P.O. Box 120   *AC: GR III, 34*
French Camp, MS 39745
Paul and Donna Perkins, Hosts

RATES:	**Budget**
LATITUDE/LONGITUDE:	**N 33 18'39" W 89 25'02"**
INTERNET ACCESS:	**From phone in common area**
WEB SITE:	**www.frenchcamp.org**
E-MAIL:	**fcainfo@frenchcamp.org**
RESERVATION INFO:	**(662) 547-6835; if no answer, call:**
	(662) 547-6482
FAX:	**(662) 547-6790**

One of only three inns located directly adjacent to the current Great River Route—Mamie's Cabin at the Dupree House near Raymond, Mississippi, and Bust's Cycling Hostel in Potosi, Missouri, are the others—French Camp Academy Bed & Breakfast was built to accommodate family members visiting students at the French Camp Academy (FCA). There are a total of five accommodations, three in the main house and two more in the country cabin, all with private bath. A full breakfast is served in the dining room of the main house. B&B guests are also invited to partake of lunch and dinner with the students, faculty, and staff in the FCA main dining hall on the main campus for $3 per person. The Council House Café, also run by the FCA, is just a few steps away from the inn.

Due to its affiliation with the FCA, this B&B has much to offer, including camping, horse stables, extensive mountain bike trails, a fishing lake, swimming, and—last but not least—a first class astronomy program which includes a planetarium and an observatory. It is obvious that everyone associated with the French Camp Academy is extremely proud of the installation and eager to show the facilities to visitors. If you wish to make your visit even more informative, contact Jim Hill, Director of the Rainwater Observatory, French Camp Academy, (662) 547-6865 or 6970.

Jim's email address is jhill@astronomers.org and the web site is www.rainwater.astronomers.org.

In addition to the normal school year activities, the FCA also hosts a very popular summer school. Because of these demands, it is always a prudent idea to call ahead for reservations. The staff will do their utmost to accommodate all travelers either in the B&B or by allowing on-site camping.

Cycling from French Camp Academy B&B
There are many singletrack trails on the FCA property. Except for the Trace, riding the local roads can be a bit hairy due to traffic. The inn's front door is about 300 yards in a straight line from the Trace.

Directions to French Camp Academy B&B
Both north- and southbounders must exit the NTP at MM 180, French Camp exit, onto MS 407 East. Turn left at the first inter-section (about 300 yards from the NTP) onto unmarked Bluebird Lane. There will be a French Camp B&B sign at this intersection pointing to the left.

Jim's Cabin Rental

P.O. Box 17952
Natchez, MS 39122
Jim Shelby, Host

AC: GR III, 40

RATES:	**Budget - Moderate**
LATITUDE/LONGITUDE:	**N 31 43' 31" W 91 13' 48"**
INTERNET ACCESS:	**From the guest cabin. The Natchez AOL node is a local call.**
RESERVATION INFO:	**(601) 442-1456**

This inn's style can best be described as "Jim Shelby Eclectic." Jim is constantly building on his property, and over the past several years has furnished his guest cabin with primitive antiques, an all-wood interior, and a cozy wood burning stove. Guests make their own breakfast in the well-equipped kitchen.

The property is located in a rustic setting, with ponds and a creek. Evidently, this creek was a very popular campsite for Native Americans in earlier centuries, as Jim reports finding many arrowheads along its banks.

If you do not have any sort of motorized transportation, forget about going out for dinner. The closest thing to a restaurant is Jim's kitchen. If you are northbound, be sure to stock up on a few dinner supplies while coming through Natchez. If you are a southbound rider, you must think about dinner far in advance, since there are precious few opportunities to get supplies on the Trace between Port Gibson and Church Hill. If you're really stuck, ask Jim if you can borrow his pickup to make a run for supplies or dinner.

Cycling from Jim's Cabin Rental

The area between Jim's property and the Natchez Trace is a tangled network of shaded and sunken gravel roads—great for a mountain bike, but rough on a road bike. The one road loop beginning at Jim's Cabin Rental brings you down onto the Trace

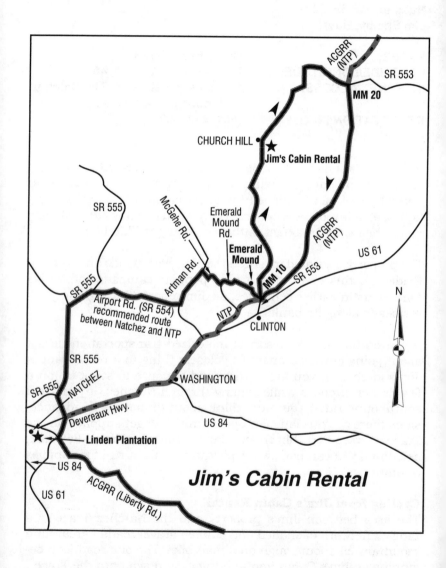

Jim's Cabin Rental

and provides an opportunity to visit the Locust Grove pioneer home site (AC: GR III, 40). Be sure to chat with the Locust Grove Ranger Eric Chamberlain, whose family lived on this very homestead from the late 1700s to the 1940s.

24-mile tour to Locust Grove and the Emerald Mound

0.0	Begin: Jim's Cabin Rental in Church Hill on SR 553. Proceed north on 553.
5.7	Right onto the Natchez Trace Parkway.
16.0	At MM 10 turn right onto SR 553. Continue straight onto Emerald Mound Rd.
16.5	Emerald Mound. Retrace route back to SR 553.
17.0	Left onto SR 553.
24.0	Finish: Jim's Cabin Rental.

Directions to Jim's Cabin Rental

Jim's Cabin Rental is located in the hamlet of Church Hill, Mississippi, about 20 miles northeast of Natchez. Describing Church Hill as a hamlet is being rather generous—it is really nothing more than a hill on which a church was built. Besides the church and a rather dilapidated (and only sporadically open) general store across the street, Jim's Cabin Rental is all there is to Church Hill.

Northbounders coming from Natchez via the Emerald Mound back road route (see page 193—The Natchez Bypass) must turn left onto SR 553 North for seven miles to Church Hill. Jim's property lies directly opposite the church. Southbounders must exit the Natchez Trace Parkway at MM 20 and bear right onto SR 553 South for six miles to Church Hill. From this direction, Jim's will be on your left, opposite the rather impressive church.

Linden, Natchez, Mississippi

Linden

One Linden Place
Natchez, MS 39120
Jeanette Feltus, Host

AC: GR III, 41

RATES:	**Moderate - Deluxe**
LATITUDE/LONGITUDE:	**N 31 40' 35" W 91 34'46"**
INTERNET ACCESS:	**From phone in the common area.** **This is an extension of the main** **house phone.**
WEB SITE:	**www.natchezms.com/linden**
RESERVATION INFO:	**(800) 2-LINDEN**
FAX:	**(601) 442-7548**

Linden was originally constructed in 1800 with three rooms. The plantation was purchased by the Feltus family in 1849, and has remained in the family ever since. In fact, the children of Innkeeper Jeanette Feltus are the sixth generation of Feltuses to live there.

The picturesque antebellum setting is particularly striking during the Christmas season, when period decorations are used to adorn every room and mantelpiece in the inn. The seven guestrooms are large and very cozy, featuring canopied fourposter beds. Several rooms open up onto a spacious sitting porch. In addition, the inn features one of the finest collections of Federal furniture in the South. The full southern breakfast, served in the formal dining room, is a palatial affair, befitting the inn whose main entrance was the inspiration for the plantation home in the epic film *Gone with the Wind.*

Linden is such an appealing place to pass the time that at least one former resident seems never to have left. An uncle—an invalid—lived in the house for years. Prior to his passing, he often walked around the property in the evenings, supported by a cane which made a very distinctive sound. Guests and staff have repeatedly observed the old man making his rounds of the property, while others have only heard the unmistakable sound of his cane tapping the ground. The cane still hangs in the main entrance hall.

It is barely a mile to the downtown area, where visitors will find a broad selection of restaurants and antique shops. The real touristy part of town is at the bottom of the bluff along the river. Times have changed, so it may be difficult to imagine that, in the late 1700s and early 1800s, this was one of the most notorious ports on the Mississippi River—if not *the* most.

Cycling from Linden

Linden is very conveniently located less than two miles from the Great River Route and equidistant from the high bluff overlooking the Mississippi River. The nearest bike shop is the Natchez Bicycle Center, 334 Main Street, (601) 446-7794, less than one mile away in the downtown area. While there are no formal local loops suggested, one should take the time for a short ride through downtown and continue on to the bluff, which offers a unique and magnificent view of the Mississippi River.

Directions to Linden

If northbound on Liberty Road, continue straight across US 61 for about one mile. Liberty will become East Franklin. Turn left (south) onto Melrose. (This will be a rather sharp turn and, due to one-way conditions, might require you to push the bike onto the sidewalk to make the turn.) Linden will be on your left after about 200 yards. This location is less than two miles from the river.

To regain the northbound route, turn right out of Linden and retrace your route to the first big intersection. Make an easy right onto Devereaux for one mile to Linda Lee. Turn left onto Linda Lee West for one mile to Martin Luther King. Turn Right onto Martin Luther King North and follow the instructions for the Natchez bypass, page 193.

If coming into town southbound on the recommended Natchez Bypass along Martin Luther King and Linda Lee, turn right onto

Devereaux for less than one mile. Where Devereaux becomes one way, bear right onto St. Catherine for about three tenths of a mile and then turn left onto Junkin and a rather steep downhill. Upon crossing East Franklin, Junkin becomes Melrose. Continue straight on Melrose and Linden will be on your left after about 200 yards.

If coming into town on the original Great River Route along US 61, continue straight onto the Devereaux highway and follow the instructions in the paragraph immediately above.

For those continuing southbound on the Great River Route, upon departing Linden turn right onto Melrose to the first big intersection. Make a hard right onto Liberty Road for less than one mile to US 61. Continue straight across US 61 and you will rejoin the original Great River Route at that intersection.

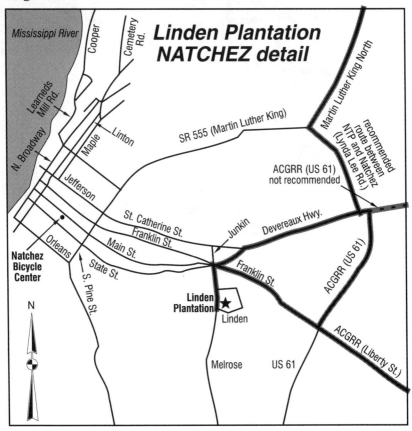

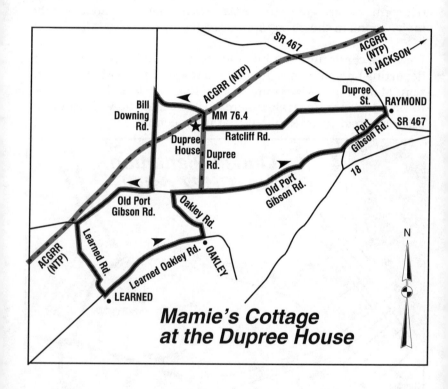

**Mamie's Cottage
at the Dupree House**

Mamie's Cottage at the Dupree House

2809 Dupree Road (Opposite MM 76 on the Trace)
Raymond, MS 39154
Brenda & Charles Davis, Hosts   *AC: GR III, 38*

RATES:	**Budget (Kids under 12 free)**
LATITUDE/LONGITUDE:	**N 32 15' 31" W 90 30' 14"**
INTERNET ACCESS:	**From guestroom**
WEB SITE:	**www.raymondms.com/tour10.htm**
EMAIL:	**cdavis@mdot.state.ms.us**
RESERVATION INFO:	**(877) 629-6051**
FAX:	**(601) 857-3136**

The Dupree House is one of a handful of inns located directly adjacent to the Natchez Trace and Great River Route. The main house was built in 1850 in the Transitional Greek Revival Italianate style. A Dr. Dupree expanded the building in 1878. In the early 1990s, the current owners moved a typical planter's cottage—Greek revival with undercut gallery—to the property from Raymond and named it Mamie's Cottage after the doctor's adopted daughter. The two guest suites are located in Mamie's Cottage: one named for Pattie Dupree and the other for owner Charles Davis's aunt, Madge Davis-Jones, who provided immense support for the renovation.

Brenda and Charles Davis are only the fourth family to occupy the main house since its construction. It had been boarded up for a decade prior to being purchased by the Davises, helping to protect the house from vandalism and preserving much of the home's original character. In fact, seventy percent of the glass panes throughout the building are original. Thanks to its pristine and unaltered condition, the Dupree House has a distinct character and cheerful ambience. The innkeepers feel that the Dupree family presence is still very much in evidence.

Brenda serves a delicious country breakfast. With sufficient notice, she can produce a wonderful meal at another time of the day for an additional—but very reasonable—fee. In Raymond, one has a choice of several fast food restaurants.

Cycling from Mamie's Cottage
With light rollers, tree shaded back roads, and quaint country hamlets, this is a very pleasant area for cycling. The 26-mile local loop takes riders through the hamlets of Learned and Raymond. The nearest bike shop is about 25 miles away:

> Indian Cycle Fitness & Outdoor
> I-55N & County Line Road
> Jackson, MS
> (601) 956-8383

26-mile tour to Learned and Raymond
0.0	Begin: Dupree House. Proceed left on Dupree Rd. West
1.6	Left onto Bill Downing Rd.
4.6	Right onto the Old Port Gibson Rd.
7.0	Left onto the Learned Rd.
9.0	Pass through hamlet of Learned. Turn left onto Learned Oakley Rd.
12.0	At Oakley turn left onto Oakley Rd.
14.0	Right onto the Old Port Gibson Rd.
19.0	Left onto the Port Gibson Rd.
21.0	Raymond village center. Left onto SR 467
21.2	Left onto Dupree St. (becomes Ratliff Rd.)
26.0	Right onto Dupree Rd.
26.3	Finish: Dupree House

Directions to Mamie's Cottage
Southbound: Continue to MM 76.4 where you encounter a concrete bridge. Rather than cross the bridge, bear right though the grass to DuPree Road below, being careful to avoid any obstacles installed to prevent unauthorized motor traffic onto and off of the Trace. Once off the Trace, turn left, passing under the bridge. The entrance to the DuPree House, just around the curve on your right, is well marked. If you find no signs, you have taken the wrong bridge off the Trace.

Northbound: Look for mile MM 76, which is 10 miles north of the SR 27 exit. The DuPree House will be on the right. If you do not wish to cross through the field to the house, continue on to the bridge at MM 76.4. Cross over the southbound lane and exit down to the left onto DuPree Road, being careful to avoid any obstacles designed to prevent unauthorized motor traffic onto and off of the Trace. Once down on DuPree Road follow the instructions above.

Note: If you have a cell phone or can somehow call ahead, the innkeepers will gladly meet you on the Trace and guide you to the inn, which can actually be seen just east of the Trace from late autumn through early spring. During the remainder of the year, the inn is blocked by foliage.

For those travelers who prefer to take the regular paved route from the Trace, at MM 78 take the SR 467 exit east into Raymond. Just after entering the village, turn right onto DuPree Street for about four and a half miles. At the T turn right onto DuPree Road for about three tenths of a mile and the DuPree House will be on your left just as the road curves to the left under the Trace. If you go under the Trace you have gone too far.

Millsaps Buie House, Jackson, Mississippi

Millsaps Buie House

628 North State Street
Jackson, MS 39202
Judy Fenters, Host

AC: GR III, 37

RATES:	**Budget - Deluxe**
LATITUDE/LONGITUDE:	**N 32 18' 47" W 90 11' 13"**
INTERNET ACCESS:	**From guest room**
WEB SITE:	**www.millsapsbuiehouse.com**
E-MAIL:	**Info@MillsapsBuieHouse.com**
RESERVATION INFO:	**(800) 784-0221 or (601) 352-0221**

Civil War veteran Rueben Webster Millsaps, entrepreneur and philanthropist, built this classic three-story Victorian mansion in 1888. Major Millsaps played a significant role in restarting commerce—as well as academic and religious life—in his home state of Mississippi after the war. The nearby Methodist college which he founded bears his name.

Listed on the National Register of Historic Places, the Millsaps Buie House boasts a formal dining room, parlor, and eleven accommodations furnished with every imaginable luxury. But the opulent furnishings are only one element of the inn's attractiveness. On the epicurian level, the management seems to have a wonderful preference for fresh fruit. It is everywhere, included even in the arrival snack.

But wait until you experience the breakfast. While the brochures indicate a full southern breakfast, that description simply does not do it justice. With huge amounts of fresh fruit, stacks of pastries, French toast, waffles, omelets of every imaginable variety, cheese grits, scrambled eggs, and thick slices of ham, the Millsaps Buie House breakfast was, undoubtedly, one of the most spectacular culinary productions encountered on this tour.

Cycling from Millsaps Buie House

One way or another, the touring cyclist must deal with the city of Jackson, Mississippi, either by going directly through it or by-passing it. Though one will encounter less traffic overall on the bypass, you will forego the opportunity to view the State Capitol and miss a visit to the Fairview Inn or Millsaps Buie House. In spite of being an urban center with lots of rush hour traffic, the local drivers seemed yielding and friendly.

The terrain along the tree-shaded back streets is quite hilly in spots. Nevertheless, this inn regularly hosts large cycling groups and provides secure bicycle storage on the enclosed back porch. From the front desk, round the clock security monitors the house and grounds.

There are at least two very good, full service bike shops in Jackson:

> The Bike Rack (six miles to the east)
> 5050 Parkway Drive
> (in the Colonial Mart Shopping Center)
> Jackson MS 39211
> (601) 956-6891
>
> Indian Cycle Shop (seven miles due north and very easy to reach via the mid-town route)
> 1060 East County Line Road
> Ridgeland MS 39157
> (601) 956-8383

Directions to Millsaps Buie House

For detailed instructions on the Jackson Mid-City route to both inns as well as the bypass route, see page 194. Also see the Jackson detail map on page 129.

Mockingbird Inn Bed & Breakfast

305 North Gloster Street
Tupelo, MS 38804
Sharon Robertson, Host

AC: GR II, 30

RATES:	**Budget - Moderate**
LATITUDE/LONGITUDE:	**N 34 15' 34" W 88 42' 57"**
WEB SITE:	**www.bbonline.com/ms/mockingbird**
E-MAIL:	**Sandbird@netbird.com**
RESERVATION PHONE:	**(662) 841-0286**
FAX:	**(662) 840-4158**

Tupelo's main attraction, of course, is Elvis Presley, whose presence dominates the area. He attended 6th and 7th grades at the Milam elementary school, located right across the street from the Mockingbird Inn. His birthplace (306 Elvis Presley Drive) is less than three miles from the inn.

The cheerful, two-story Mockingbird Inn was a private home from the time it was built in 1925 until 1955. Since then it has been a ladies clothing boutique, a patio store, and an apartment building before finally becoming a bed & breakfast inn in 1993. There are seven very comfortable accommodations based on national and international themes, including Germany, France, Africa, Venice, Athens, Sanibel Island, and Mackinaw Island. An enclosed porch enhances the down home ambience.

Befitting its role as a refuge from the worries of the world at large, the Mockingbird has been miraculously spared by Mother Nature's wrath on more than one occasion. In 1936, when a devastating tornado laid waste to Tupelo, this house was untouched and actually used as a hospital. And the house was again completely spared during a major ice storm in 1994 that knocked out power and heat throughout Tupelo.

A full breakfast is served from 7am to 8:30am during the week, and a bit later on weekends. Plenty of dining options are nearby;

the closest restaurant, JP's, is barely 100 yards away to the west on Jefferson. The Cancun Mexican restaurant is not much further away on North Gloster. Several fast food restaurants are within walking distance of the inn.

You don't have to take my word that the Mockingbird is one of the finest inns in the area; the Mockingbird Inn has been rated in the *Top Ten Best Bed & Breakfasts in Mississippi* and featured in, among others, *America's Best Bed & Breakfasts, South's Best Bed & Breakfasts, Inside Mississippi, Traveling the Trace*, and *America's Wonderful Little Hotels & Inns*.

Cycling from the Mockingbird Inn

This location is about four miles from the Natchez Trace Parkway. If there's no room at the inn, and you like to camp, try the free hiker/biker campground near the Tupelo Visitor Center. Camping is also available at the Elvis Presley Park.

The ride from the Mockingbird to the Presley home at 306 Elvis Presley Drive, a distance of less than three miles, is very simple. Just follow these cues:

0.0   Begin at the Mockingbird and proceed east on Jefferson
        Street
0.8   Right onto Commerce South
0.9   Left onto SR 6 (Main Street) East
2.1   Left onto Elvis Presley Drive North
2.2   Finish at Presley home at 306 Elvis Presley Drive

There are two bike shops in Tupelo:

> The Bike Shop
> Mike Olmstead
> 1143 West Main
> Tupelo MS 38804
> (601) 842-7341

This shop is on the main road into Tupelo about three miles east of the Natchez Trace on the south side of the road. It's about a mile from the inn.

The Bicycle Paceline
Brian Piaza
2120 West Jackson Rd
Tupelo MS 38804
(601) 844-8660
bicyclep@tsixroads.com

This shop is immediately west of the Trace on the North side of West Jackson, about four miles from the inn. While there is no formal exit onto West Jackson, it is possible to push the bike across the grass and down onto the road. Jackson Road is the first overpass north of the US 6 exit and one overpass south of the Tupelo Visitor's Center.

Directions to the Mockingbird Inn

The Mockingbird is less than three miles from the Natchez Trace Parkway. Riders from either direction should exit at MM 260 onto SR 6 East for 2.2 miles. **Note:** SR 6 is a very busy road and one must exercise extreme caution. Turn left at Rankin Boulevard for one long block to Jefferson Street. Turn right onto Jefferson for three short blocks and the Mockingbird will be on the left at the intersection of Jefferson and North Gloster.

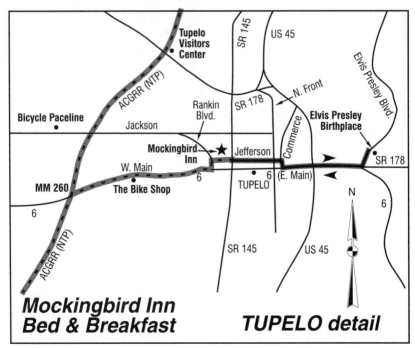

*Mockingbird Inn
Bed & Breakfast*

TUPELO detail

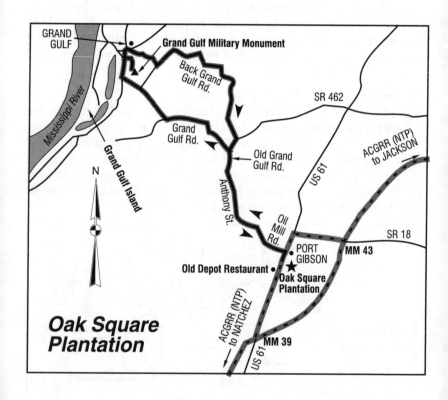

GRAND GULF

Grand Gulf Military Monument

Back Grand Gulf Rd.

SR 462

Mississippi River

Grand Gulf Rd.

Old Grand Gulf Rd.

ACGRR (NTP) to JACKSON

Grand Gulf Island

US 61

N

Anthony St.

Oil Mill Rd.

SR 18

MM 43

PORT GIBSON

Old Depot Restaurant ●

★ **Oak Square Plantation**

ACGRR (NTP) to NATCHEZ

Oak Square Plantation

MM 39

US 61

Oak Square Plantation

1207 Church Street
Port Gibson, MS 39150   *AC: GR III, 39*
Mrs. William D. Lum, Host

RATES:	**Moderate**
LATITUDE/LONGITUDE:	**N 31 57' 46" W 90 59' 28"**
INTERNET ACCESS:	**From guest room phone**
WEB SITE:	**www.virtualcities.com/ons/ms/w/**
	msw3601.htm
RESERVATION INFO:	**(800) 729-0240**
FAX:	**(601) 437-5768**

Oak Square Plantation is a classic Greek Revival mansion straight out of the pages of *Gone with the Wind*. Originally constructed in 1850, Oak Square has been in the same family for decades. Each of the nine double room accommodations are equipped with modern conveniences like air conditioning, television, and telephone, as well as authentic 18th- and 19th-century furnishings. Many of these pieces are original to the house or gathered from the innkeeper's family; ask Mrs. Lum for a tour of the grounds and the stories behind the many family heirlooms.

A full southern breakfast is served on the enclosed sun porch. For other meals, try The Old Depot Restaurant, (601) 437-4711, a pleasantly short two-and-a-half block stroll away at the intersection of China and Main Streets.

The Civil War lives on in Port Gibson, a town described by Ulysses S. Grant as "too beautiful to burn." A visit to the nearby Grand Gulf State Park and Battlefield—the site of one of General Grant's few defeats—is well worth staying an extra day.

Cycling from Oak Square Plantation

The local loop, partially along sunken roads, takes you right to the Grand Gulf military park. Oak Square is quite a distance—about 40 miles—from the closest bicycle repair facility, the Natchez Bicycle Center. Secure bicycle parking is available.

20-mile tour to Grand Gulf State Park and Battlefield

0.0	Begin: Port Gibson at intersection of China St. and US 61, adjacent to Oak Square Plantation. Proceed north on US 61
0.6	Left at the light onto Oil Mill Rd., which becomes Anthony St. and later Old Grand Gulf Rd.
4.2	Left onto Grand Gulf Rd.
9.0	Grand Gulf Military Park
9.2	Right onto unnamed road. (**Note:** Due to the lack of named roads, it is recommended to ask for specific directions to this connection at the Grand Gulf Military Museum. The day I visited the museum, folks could not have been more helpful.)
10.2	Left onto Back Grand Gulf Rd.
15.4	Right onto Old Grand Gulf Rd.
19.4	Right onto US 61
20.0	Finish: Port Gibson at intersection of China St. and US 61

Directions to Oak Square Plantation

Port Gibson lies astride US 61, 28 miles south of Vicksburg and 40 miles north of Natchez. The Trace runs about one mile to the east of Port Gibson. If northbound, exit the Natchez Trace Parkway at MM 39 onto US 61 north for one mile; Oak Square Plantation will be on the right.

If southbound, exit the Natchez Trace Parkway at MM 43 onto SR 18 west for 1.7 miles to the intersection with US 61. Turn left onto 61 South for one mile into Port Gibson; Oak Square Plantation will be on the left.

Rosswood Plantation

RR 1 Box 6
Lorman, MS 39096-9703   *AC: GR III, 40*
Jean & Walt Hylander, Hosts

RATES:	**Moderate**
LATITUDE/LONGITUDE:	**N 31 48' 43" W 91 0' 11"**
INTERNET ACCESS:	**From the guest room. Extension of main house phone.**
WEB SITE:	**www.rosswood.net**
E-MAIL:	**whylander@aol.com**
RESERVATION INFO:	**(800) 533-5889**

Rosswood Plantation is a splendidly restored Greek Revival mansion originally built in 1857 for Dr. Walter Ross Wade. It is difficult to imagine the house in any but its present state, but the plantation had suffered decades of neglect by the time it was purchased by Army Colonel and former attaché Walt Hylander and his wife Jean in 1975. Now meticulously restored, the plantation's condition has improved considerably, and welcomes guests with four upstairs guestrooms furnished with period antiques including canopied beds.

In addition to renovating and maintaining the property in top condition, Walt Hylander has expended considerable effort to research the plantation's history. Among the numerous documents in his possession is the original owner's diary describing life during the antebellum period.

During the Civil War, "The Battle of the Cotton Bales" took place close by. Hylander learned that, in the course of the engagement, a Union Cohorn mortar shell blasted Rosswood's kitchen to smithereens. Over a century later, while excavating ground for the swimming pool, Colonel Hylander found the remains of that same errant shell which had destroyed the kitchen. After a bit of research, he was even able to discover not only the name of the unit, but even the name of the battery commander who fired the shell.

He also learned that the original mistress of the mansion, Mabella Wade, supposedly buried expensive silverware and other family treasures somewhere on the grounds to prevent seizure by federal troops. Hylander used a metal detector to search the immediate area around the mansion, but Mabella Wade's treasure remains buried somewhere on the property.

Twelve years after the end of the Civil War, the original owners sold the property to a spinster niece of Jefferson Davis, who lived there from 1877 to 1903. At that point, a local entrepreneur bought the property to raise fighting gamecocks. Later, the property reverted back to a cotton plantation while four sharecropping families lived in the mansion.

In 1947, 90 years after its construction, World War II veteran Daniel Mason began restoring the mansion by installing electricity and plumbing. Unfortunately, a lack of funds soon brought restoration efforts to a halt. By 1950, Rosswood had become the summer home for a large New Orleans family who later abandoned the property in the early 1970s.

Today, things are as peaceful as they've ever been at Rosswood Plantation. Balmy summer evenings will often find guests and hosts chatting around the swimming pool or spa. The Hylanders are very gracious hosts, and their background probably has something to do with that. As the spouse of an attaché, Jean devoted much time to hosting diplomatic functions at U.S. embassies and Officers' Wives Clubs. They have successfully transferred those experiences to their current vocation.

The Old Country Store in Lorman, three miles away, is the best choice for dining out. The restaurant has shed its former country store image and has become rather upscale. The Old Depot in Port Gibson is the next-closest restaurant, 16 miles away. If you anticipate a late afternoon or early evening arrival, Jean Hylander suggests dinner at the The Old Country Store, or stopping in Port Gibson to purchase dinner supplies to bring with you to the plantation in order to avoid riding the local roads in the darkness.

Cycling from Rosswood Plantation

The local loop will take you on very pretty back roads to Canemount Plantation, the Windsor Ruins, and Port Gibson. At Port Gibson, the loop takes the Natchez Trace Parkway back to the exit at MM 30 and the return to Rosswood.

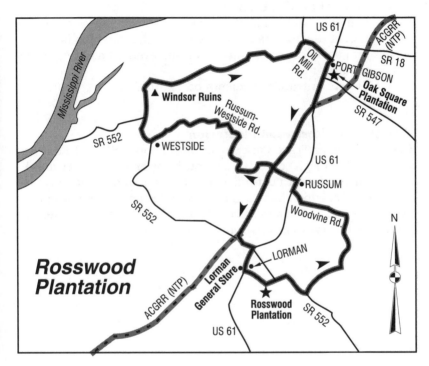

52-mile tour to the Windsor Ruins, Port Gibson, and Lorman's ex-General Store

0.0	Begin: entrance to Rosswood Plantation. Proceed east on SR 552.
1.0	Left onto first paved road. Eventually becomes Woodvine Rd.
9.5	Right onto US 61 North
9.6	Left onto Russum/Westside Rd.
20.6	Right onto SR 552
21.9	Where SR 552 bends sharply to the left, continue straight to the Windsor Ruins
24.0	Pass entrance to Windsor Ruins. Continue towards Port Gibson

34.0   In Port Gibson, bear right onto Carroll St. East
34.3   Right onto US 61 South
36.8   Right onto the NTP access road and then left onto the NTP South
46.8   Exit off the NTP onto SR 552 East
48.0   Right onto US 61 South
49.0   Left onto SR 552. (**_Note:_** This intersection is also the location of the famous Lorman General Store, which is a general store no longer but has re-incarnated as an upscale restaurant
52.0   Finish: entrance to Rosswood Plantation

Directions to Rosswood Plantation

Exit the Natchez Trace Parkway at MM 30 onto SR 552 East for one mile. Turn right onto US 61 South for one mile to Lorman. There you will find a post office and the remains of the Lorman General Store, which has been re-incarnated as an upscale country restaurant. At Lorman, turn left onto SR 552 East. After about three miles, Rosswood will appear on your left.

Bellevue Bed & Breakfast

312 Bellevue Street
Cape Girardeau, MO 63701   *AC: GR I, 15*
Dr. Marsha Toll, Host

RATES:	**Budget - Moderate**
LATITUDE/LONGITUDE:	**N 37 18' 27" W 89 31' 17"**
INTERNET ACCESS:	**From phone in common area.**
	There are also copier and fax
	machines available for guest use.
WEB SITE:	**www.bbonline.com/mo/bellevue**
E-MAIL:	**BellevueBB@compuserve.com**
RESERVATION INFO:	**(800) 768-6822 or (573) 335-3302**

The Bellevue Bed & Breakfast was constructed in 1891 by Civil War veteran Heinrich Hunze, whose family occupied the home until 1955. At that point, the Queen Anne-style Victorian became an apartment house for university students. During renovation in the early 1990s, restorers were able to save the original pocket doors, woodwork and stained glass over the entrance door. The ceiling stencils are reproductions of the originals found hidden under layers of wallpaper.

In 1993 the restored home was reincarnated as a B&B, featuring four accommodations, each with a private bath. Dr. Marsha Toll (Ph.D. in psychology) purchased the Bellevue in mid-1999. Though she is a first-time owner, the St. Louis native gained valuable experience while running inns for the absentee owners of other inns; she had so much fun doing it she decided to acquire one of her own. At the Bellevue, she has certainly achieved her goal of creating a warm, comfortable, serene family atmosphere. Toll resides on the premises, and is ably assisted by laid-back house beagles Arthur and Beatrice.

Marsha takes great pride in her full breakfast. Served in the formal dining room, the meal features fresh breads and fruit. For other dining options, the Bellevue is only a short stroll on foot from the restored downtown area of Cape Girardeau. There you will find several nice restaurants, the closest being the New Orleans. Since eateries come and go, ask the innkeeper about to the current restaurant scene.

Secure bicycle storage is provided in the garage.

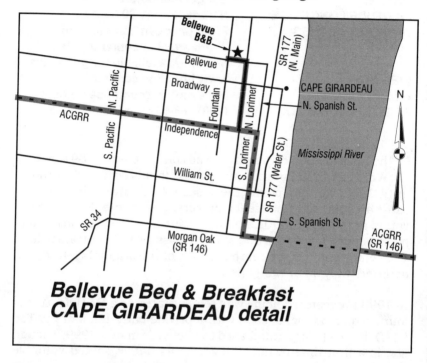

Bellevue Bed & Breakfast
CAPE GIRARDEAU detail

Cycling from the Bellevue

Because of the bridge's condition and narrow construction, getting into and out of Cape Girardeau via the Mississippi River bridge can be a white knuckle experience. Eric Gooden, owner of Cape Bicycling, has offered to provide to passing cyclists a limited shuttle service across the bridge in either direction—if he's not too busy in the shop.

Having said that, please note that a new Mississippi River bridge is currently under construction immediately adjacent to the narrow bridge. Given the progress of construction, it should be done around 2002 and will, by all accounts, include a bicycle lane.

Due to the severity of the impending hills and heavy local logging truck traffic, and also because there are few bicycle shops for miles and miles in any direction, it is absolutely necessary for anyone heading into the hills northwest out of Cape Girardeau to stop by Cape Bicycles for a quick check up of brakes, cables, and tires. This stretch between Cape Girardeau and St. Louis might well be the greatest cycling challenge many cyclists have ever encountered. Make sure to carry a spare of everything and ride this segment only if you are experienced or in the company of experienced cyclists.

To avoid the Missouri hills, The Marquardt Trail (page 200) offers an alternative—and flat—route into St. Louis from Golconda via Prairie du Rocher, Illinois.

Local Bike Shop
Cape Bicycling & Fitness
2410 William
Cape Girardeau, MO 63701
(573) 335-2453

Directions to the Inn
Northbound: After crossing the Mississippi bridge, turn right onto Spanish Street North. Turn left onto Independence West for one block. Turn right onto Lorimer North for three blocks. Turn left onto Bellevue West; the inn will be just a few yards down on your right.

Southbound: At mile 28.5 on the AC map #15, turn left onto Independence East. After about 2.5 miles, turn left onto S. Lorimer North for three blocks to Bellevue Street. Turn left onto Bellevue Street East; the inn will be just a few yards down on your right.

Bust's Bicycle Touring Hostel, Potosi, Missouri

Bust's Bicycle Touring Hostel

612 East High Street
Potosi, MO 63664   *AC: GR I, 11*
Eli Bust, Host

RATES:	**Budget**
LATITUDE/LONGITUDE:	**N 37 55' 54" W 90 46' 47"**
INTERNET ACCESS:	**From kitchen phone**
EMAIL:	**Bust@usmo.com**
RESERVATION INFO:	**(573) 438-4457**

Adventure Cycling's Great Rivers Route cuts through Potosi's southeast quadrant. In this key location, immediately adjacent to the route, you'll find Eli Bust's Bicycle Touring Hostel, providing a welcome respite from those horrific Missouri hills.

The comfortable, two-story home was built by Eli's grandmother, Lucy McReady Bust, in 1909 and has remained in the family ever since. It was unoccupied from 1986 to 1993, when it reincarnated as a Bed & Breakfast inn—and lately, as a cyclist's hostel—with four comfortable upstairs accommodations. The home is totally authentic and the innkeeper has kept much of her grandmother's original furnishings.

A full breakfast is served in the formal dining room. If you're looking for a formal meal, the Lakeview Restaurant & Lounge, (573) 438-LAKE, is just a few blocks away in downtown Potosi. If you're the informal type but still need to get out for dinner, there is a Sonic Drive-in directly across the street from the inn and several other fast food restaurants in the area.

For most of the 18th century—even when the area was under Spanish rule, and later, after the American victory in the Revolutionary War—French was the dominant culture in this part of Missouri. In 1798, a Connecticut miner, Moses Austin, opened a general store and helped establish Missouri's first major mining and smelting industry. His son, Stephen F. Austin, grew up in

Potosi and served in the Missouri Territorial legislature as a representative from Washington County. Later, Stephen moved to the Southwest and came to be known as the Father of Texas.

The French influence is still very evident in the La Fete au Renault Mountain Men Rendevous and Black Powder Shoot, held every spring in Old Mines near Potosi, where many of the participants speak French.

Directions to Bust's Bicycle Touring Hostel
If northbound on SR P, you must turn left onto SR 8 West. Bust's Bicycle Touring Hostel will be on your right at the very next intersection of SR 8 and East Casey Street. If southbound, just look for the Sonic Drive-in on your right as you leave Potosi. The hostel will be on your left, directly opposite the Sonic.

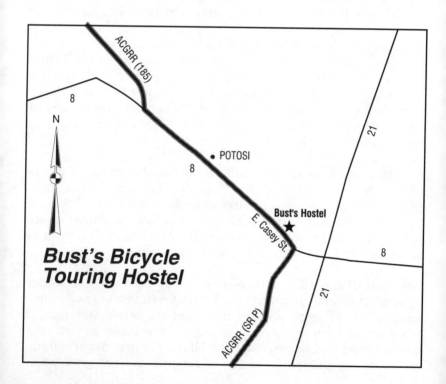

Lafayette House Bed & Breakfast

2156 Lafayette Avenue
St. Louis, MO 63104   *AC: GR I, St. Louis Spur*
Nancy Hammersmith, Host

RATES:	**Budget - Moderate**
LATITUDE/LONGITUDE:	**N 38 36'35" W 90 13' 49"**
INTERNET ACCESS:	**From guestroom phone**
WEB SITE:	**www.bbonline.com/mo/lafayette**
RESERVATION INFO:	**(800) 641-8965 or (314) 772-4429**
FAX:	**(314) 664-2156**

During the Civil War, Captain James Eads constructed the seven ironclad warships that were so effective in winning the river war. Later, he turned his talents to a more constructive area and, in addition to building a home for each of his four daughters, erected the famous Eads bridge across the Mississippi, which is still in active use. One of the homes that he built for his daughters is now the Lafayette House Bed & Breakfast.

The classic three-story, fourteen-room Queen Anne mansion was built in 1876 by Eads as a wedding gift for his daughter Martha, who subsequently lived there from 1876-81. A tornado leveled much of the neighborhood in 1896, taking off the entire third floor of the structure and causing massive and lasting damage to this section of St. Louis. In the early 20th century the mansion became a boarding house, and the surrounding area became rather sleazy. But in 1972 the entire neighborhood was declared an historic area and has since become one of the city's gentrified neighborhoods.

In 1984 the Lafayette House began its incarnation as a B&B with seven tastefully decorated accommodations. In the living room, you will find the original walnut mantel. There is also a parlor with TV, games, books and a refrigerator stuffed with beverages. Innkeeper Nancy Hammersmith says she feels blessed that she can share her home with guests. She has created a very serene and welcoming environment at Lafayette House, while avoiding the overly frilly nature of so many inns. The B&B is easy to find on the southwest corner of Lafayette Park, just 1.5 miles from downtown and the Arch. The Lafayette House is AAA inspected and approved.

If you plan to go out for dinner, try Ricardo's restaurant, located diagonally across the park at 1931 Park Street, where guests of the Lafayette House receive a discount. Another Italian restaurant, Arcelio's, is about 200 yards further east on Park Street.

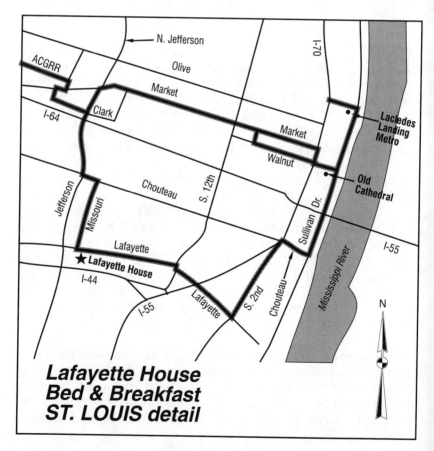

Lafayette House
Bed & Breakfast
ST. LOUIS detail

Directions to Lafayette House

Eastbound into St. Louis: At mile 6.5 on the AC St. Louis spur, turn right onto Jefferson South for less than one-half mile to Chouteau. Turn left onto Chouteau East for one block to Missouri. Turn right onto Missouri South for less than one-half mile to where it ends at Lafayette. The Lafayette House will be directly ahead on the far (south) side of Lafayette Street.

Westbound from East St. Louis, Illinois: After leaving the Metro, coast down to the river. Turn right onto Sullivan Drive South. After less than a mile turn right onto Chouteau West for just a couple of blocks and then left onto Second Street South for half a mile. Turn right onto Lafayette West for a mile and a half and the Lafayette House will be on your left. Just reverse this route to get from the inn to the Arch.

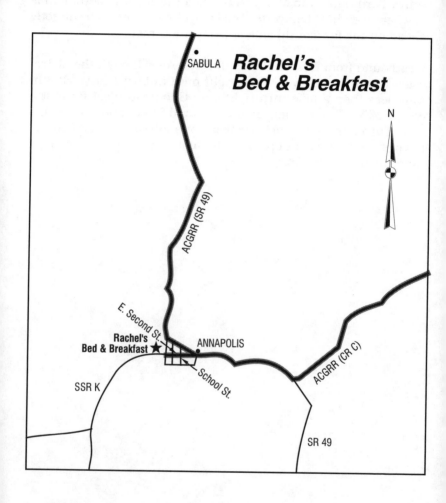

Rachel's Bed & Breakfast

202 West 2nd Street
Annapolis, MO 63620
Joe, Sharon, and Rachel Cluck, Hosts

AC: GR I, 13

RATES:	**Budget**
LATITUDE/LONGITUDE:	**N37 21' 39" W 90 41' 58"**
INTERNET ACCESS:	**From hall phone**
WEB SITE:	**www.bbonline.com/mo/rachels**
E-MAIL:	**rachelsbnb@semo.net**
RESERVATION INFO:	**(888) 245-7771**

Rachel's offers a caring and serene atmosphere. With two Registered Nurses and a former hospital administrator as hosts, you can be sure the staff at Rachel's Bed & Breakfast knows how to care for guests.

The Arts and Crafts-style building was constructed by a wealthy businessman in the 1920s, and was the first home in the area equipped with running water and electricity. Through the years it has served a variety of functions, and at one point the addition of a residential care facility substantially increased the size of the building. Joe and Sharon Cluck purchased the property in 1992 and opened their B&B operation—named after their daughter—in 1996, with seven guestrooms. The rooms are very comfortable—not overdecorated—and the whole house seems to exude a relaxed, homey atmosphere. Guests can look forward to an evening sitting around the piano in the parlor chatting with the other guests and singing songs.

A full breakfast is served in the formal dining room. The two restaurants in the hamlet are both less than 500 yards from Rachel's: The Country Cottage Inn is open Tuesday through Sunday, and the Stop Light Cafe is open seven days a week. On the off chance that both restaurants are closed, Joe and Sharon will see to it that you don't go to bed hungry. The best news is that there is a fully-equipped ice cream store right in the kitchen!

Cycling from Rachel's B&B

With continuous long and steep hills, this is undoubtedly one of the most remote and difficult areas for cyclists on the entire route between St. Louis and New Orleans. To make cycling even more interesting, there is a rather consistent stream of logging truck traffic along these back roads. Due to the combination of severely limited visibility around the tight curves and the logging and dump trucks hurtling up and down those hills, riders must exercise extreme caution when bicycling through this area.

Directions to Rachel's B&B

Northbound: Rachel's is located just a block off the Great River Road trail. As you enter Annapolis from the east on SR 49 North, rather than turning right (north) in the center of the village, continue straight onto East 2nd Street for one block to School Street. Rachel's will be on the right-hand, northwest corner of that intersection. There is a sign in front.

Southbound: As you enter Annapolis on 49 South, turn right onto East 2nd Street at that point in the middle of the village where SR 49 makes a sharp turn to the left. Follow East 2nd Street west for one block to School Street. Rachel's will on the right-hand, northwest corner of that intersection. There is a sign in front.

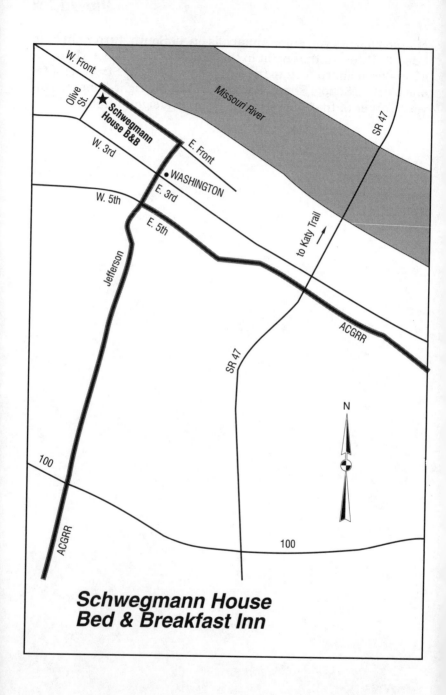

**Schwegmann House
Bed & Breakfast Inn**

Schwegmann House Bed & Breakfast Inn

438 West Front Street
Washington, MO 63090   *AC: GR I, 9*
Bill & Cathy Nagel, Hosts

RATES:	Budget - Deluxe
LATITUDE/LONGITUDE:	N 38 33' 45" W 91 0' 56"
INTERNET ACCESS:	From the guestroom
WEB SITE:	www.schwegmannhouse.com
E-MAIL ADDRESS:	cathy@schwegmannhouse.com
RESERVATION INFO:	(800) 949-2262
FAX:	(636) 239-3920

The Schwegmann House, a two-and-a-half-story structure in the Georgian Revival style, was completed in 1861 with fourteen rooms and three fireplaces. The original owner, Johann Schwegmann, was part of the wave of German immigrants who left a lasting impression on all aspects of life in the Missouri Valley. The building remained in continuous use as a private home and boarding house until Bill and Cathy Nagel purchased the property in 1983 to save it from destruction. Restoration began immediately, and six months later the Schwegmann House Bed & Breakfast opened its doors in its original 1861 configuration, featuring a panoramic view of the wide Missouri River through its Italianate front door.

Today the inn—barely a mile from the Great River Route—offers nine accommodations, each elegantly furnished with period antiques and private bath. A full breakfast is served after 7am in the dining room. For early-rising cyclists, the Nagels are happy to provide a coupon for breakfast at a nearby restaurant. Lunch and dinner is available with pre-arrangement, and there are several excellent restaurants within half a mile. Check with Bill or Cathy for the latest restaurant information.

Like many of the old inns in this book, Schwegmann House has had its share of spooky happenings. Cathy recounted how once, when she was completely alone in the house, she heard a voice clearly say "I'm glad to be back." Otherworldly or not, such a statement must be music to an innkeeper's ears!

Cycling from Schwegmann House

Due to the close proximity of the Katy Trail—barely three miles away on the opposite side of the river—visitors should seriously consider lingering an extra day or two in the Washington area to ride part of this historic 225-mile rail trail; this will be the only such opportunity available on this route. A 165-mile portion of the Katy Trail is also part of the Lewis and Clark National Historic Trail, and Daniel Boone's grave is only minutes away by bicycle, near Marthasville.

South of the Missouri River, the country roads are narrow, rolling, and have no shoulder. North of the river, the terrain is much more level. The nearest full-service bike shop is Scenic Cycles in Marthasville, about four miles away, located directly on the Katy Trail. Secure bike parking is provided on the back porch of Schwegmann House.

Directions to Schwegmann House

If northbound, you will enter Washington on Jefferson Street. Rather than turn right onto 5th Street, continue straight on Jefferson for less than three-tenths of a mile to Front Street, on the river. Turn left onto Front Street West for about six-tenths of a mile. The Schwegmann House will be on your left at the intersection of Front and Olive streets.

If southbound, turn right onto Jefferson toward the river at the intersection of 5th Street and Jefferson. Turn left onto Front Street for about six-tenths of a mile. The Schwegmann House will be on your left at the intersection of Front Street and Olive Street.

Staats-Waterford Estate Bed & Breakfast

4550 Boles Road
Labadie, MO 63005-5560   *AC: GR I, 9*
Charles Staats, Host

RATES:	**Budget**
LATITUDE/LONGITUDE:	**N 38 31' 7" W 90 53' 25"**
WEB SITE:	**www.bbim.org/staats**
RESERVATION INFO:	**(636) 451-5560**

The Staats-Waterford Estate Bed & Breakfast stands high on a hill overlooking the Missouri River Valley, less than one mile from the Great River Road St. Louis spur. Built in 1850 as a fruit and dairy farm, it remained so until 1976, when the house was renovated and indoor commodes were installed for the first time. The Greek Revival structure features a New Orleans courtyard in the center and two luxurious accommodations furnished in an 1860s theme. From the enclosed upstairs porch, there is a breathtaking view of the Missouri River Valley below. To help unwind from the rigors of the road, a carafe of local wine is normally served to arriving guests.

A veteran Civil War re-enactor, Major Charles Staats—the innkeeper—is particularly interested in the medical aspects of that period. His grandfather, Alford Hiffmann, regimental bugler of CO C, 12th Missouri, a German-speaking unit under General Franz Sigel, served four years in the Union army and kept a daily diary written in German. He participated in many campaigns, including the battle at Grand Gulf. (For a tour of the Grand Gulf battlefield, refer to page 152.)

Consequently, a visit to the Staats-Waterford estate involves much more than staying a night in a beautifully restored inn filled with period antiques. The innkeeper's intent is to take you back to the 1860s and the excitement of the Civil War period. To do so, he's been known to serve a full country breakfast dressed in the uniform of an 1861 Union army surgeon. Charles also builds and maintains a collection of Civil War rolling stock. His wagons and horses are in constant demand by movie studios and have appeared in such productions as *The Blue and the Gray* and *The Buffalo Soldiers*. Charles, a Coast Guard diver by trade, participated in raising the Eads ironclad warship *USS Cairo*, sunk during the Civil War.

The area around Labadie was settled by pioneers from Virginia City, Virginia, in 1788. In 1803, while on their outbound journey of discovery, Lewis and Clark landed at St. Albans to visit Daniel Boone at his home near Marthasville. Today, this region is best known as the heart of the Missouri wine country.

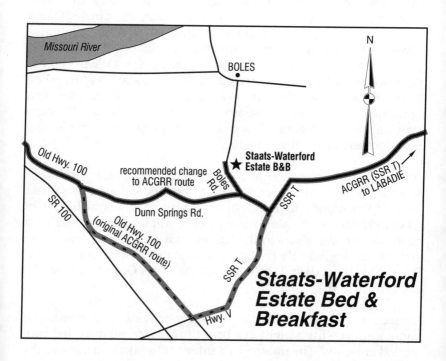

Cycling from the Staats-Waterford Estate

While the local roads are hilly, narrow, and have no paved shoulder to speak of, traffic remains generally light to medium. If necessary, Charles Staats will shuttle bikes a reasonable distance with his pickup truck. The nearest bicycle shop is Scenic Cycles in Marthasville, 14 miles away.

Directions to the Staats-Waterford Estate

If eastbound from Washington, Missouri, on the St. Louis spur, continue east on East Fifth Street. About five miles east of Washington, turn left onto Old 100 for two miles to the intersection of Old 100 and Dunn Springs Road. Turn left onto Dunn Springs Road (which is rather hilly) for 1.5 miles to the intersection with Boles Road on the left. Turn left onto Boles Road for 0.3 mile. The Staats-Waterford Estate will be on the right. The inn is easily recognized by the Civil War wagon parked in the front yard.

Westbound from St. Louis, Route T passes under a railroad trestle just west of Labadie. Exactly 1.5 miles west of that trestle, turn right onto Boles/Dunn Spring Road. After barely half a mile, follow Boles Road to the right. The Staats-Waterford Estate will be on the right after 0.3 mile.

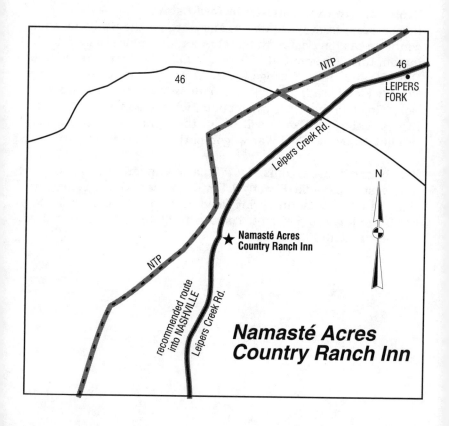

Namasté Acres Country Ranch Inn

5436 Leiper's Creek Road
Franklin, TN 37064   *AC: N/A*
Bill, Lisa, & Lindsey Winters, Hosts

RATES:	Budget
LATITUDE/LONGITUDE:	N 35 52' 46" W 87 01' 32"
INTERNET ACCESS:	From in-room phone. The Nashville AOL connection is a local call from this inn
WEB SITE:	www.bbonline.com/tn/namaste
E-MAIL:	namastebb@aol.com
RESERVATION INFO:	(615) 791-0333
FAX:	(615) 591-0665

When Bill and Lisa Winters purchased Namasté Acres in 1993, the ranch was nothing more than a house on 5 acres. Located in a scenic valley noted for upscale horse farms owned by well-known media personalities, and with direct trail connections to the horse trails paralleling the Natchez Trace Parkway, the Winters' intent was not only to provide lodging for horses and riders along the Natchez Trace, but also to board and train horses. Following an extensive renovation, Namasté Acres has become one of the leading equestrian B&Bs in the entire region. And it's also a great stopover for cyclists.

The Dutch Colonial house now offers four guestrooms, each based on a specific western or Civil War theme: Bunk House, Battle of Franklin, Native American, and Frontier Cabin. Behind the house, a swimming pool and an all-season hot tub beckon to guests. There you will also find a horse shoe pit and a fire ring for evening campfires and hot dog roasts.

Cycling from Namasté Acres
The inn's location is an easy and scenic 2.5 miles jaunt from the Natchez Trace. Indeed, Leiper's Creek Road, which passes directly in front of the ranch, is the recommended cycling route

into and out of Nashville, which is 25 miles away. This route neatly bypasses the hilliest part of the Natchez Trace Parkway. Refer to page 197, "The Nashville Spur."

The entire Franklin/Leiper's Fork area is a well-known cycling destination. It is very easy to combine the Trace with local roads to come up with loop tours along delightful back roads with great scenery and little general stores all about. The hamlet of Leiper's Fork (pop. 400), with two restaurants and an antiques shop, is barely three miles away to the north. Twelve miles away you will find Franklin, Tennessee, which is included on the National Register of Historic Places and has been voted the best small town in Tennessee. Franklin is literally bursting with great little shops (including two full-service bicycle shops), numerous unique eating establishments, and a rather significant Civil War battlefield. The local loop included in this book goes through Franklin.

The nearest bike shops are both about 13 miles from Namasté Acres in Franklin:

Lightning Cycle
120 4th Avenue South
Franklin, TN 37064
(615) 794-6050
www.lightningcycles.com

Franklin Bicycle Co.
112 Watson Glen
Franklin, TN 37064
(615) 790-2702

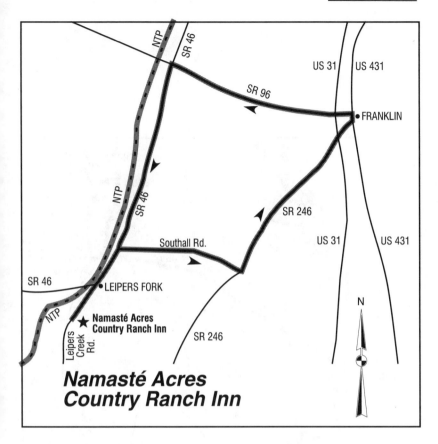

21-mile Franklin Loop

0.0	Begin: Namasté Acres and proceed north on Leiper's Creek Rd.
1.7	Straight on SR 46.
3.2	Right onto Southhall Rd.
7.4	Left onto SR 246
11.6	In the middle of Franklin, turn left onto US 431
11.7	Left onto SR 96
17.6	Left onto SR 46
19.2	Straight onto Leiper's Creek Rd.
20.9	Finish: Namasté Acres

Directions to Namasté Acres

For instructions on reaching this inn from either north or south, refer to the Nashville Spur section on page 197.

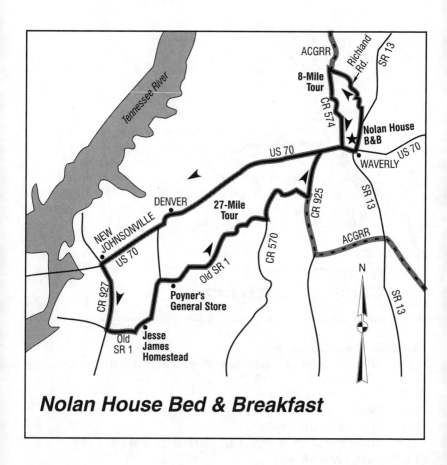

Nolan House Bed & Breakfast

Nolan House Bed & Breakfast

375 Highway 13 North
Waverly, TN 37185   *AC: GR II, 23*
Patrick Todd O'Lee, Host

RATES:	**Budget**
LATITUDE/LONGITUDE:	**N 36 5' 17" W 87 47' 35"**
INTERNET ACCESS:	**From phone in common area**
RESERVATION INFO:	**(931) 296-2511**

The Victorian-style Nolan House was built in 1870 by Lieutenant James Nicholas Nolan, an Irish immigrant and commander of the local Union garrison defending the railroad supply line into Nashville. Following the Civil War, he settled in Waverly and became one of the area's leading hoteliers. Nolan, his first two wives, and all his children are buried on the property next to the house. Nolan's third wife, Molly Blessing, was a pianist, and the musical motif in the form of a lyre is evident throughout the Inn.

Each of the three spacious guestrooms has its own entrance, as well as a private bath and fireplace. The television and telephone are located in the common sitting room.

For breakfast, Patrick Todd O'Lee, the innkeeper, serves fresh baked breads and muffins along with fresh fruit and cold cereals on English china. Be sure to ask him about the best choices for dining out. Befitting Pat's Irish heritage, one often hears soft Celtic music floating through the inn.

Also befitting his heritage, Pat is a great storyteller, and loves to talk about the history of the inn and the surrounding area. From 1878 until 1880, he says, Jesse James rented a farm near Waverly using the alias of J.D. Howard. According to local research, Jesse was called "The Rabbit Man," because he was perceived as being very timid. History has shown that, rather than being timid, he was merely going to great lengths to avoid calling any attention to himself or his family. Pat is convinced that the James boys, Jesse and Frank, both avid poker players, actually played cards in the inn's parlor.

Sometime during that period in Waverly, Jesse's wife gave birth to twin boys (Gould & Montgomery) who later succumbed to what appears to be yellow fever. The twin's remains are buried about 100 yards behind the site of the original farmhouse. According to Pat, one of the twin's gravestones is still there, the other one evidently having been removed several years ago by souvenir hunters.

The 27-mile local loop takes cyclists past the homestead. The structure currently standing on the property was a replacement for the house originally occupied by Jesse James, which later burned to the ground. The wood for the current structure was taken from the barn that Jesse rented. Unfortunately, it is private property and not open to visitors.

Other local attractions include Loretta Lynn's Dude Ranch about nine miles south of Waverly on Highway 13 and the Civil War fort erected by Lieutenant Nolan on a hill high above the village.

Cycling from The Nolan House
The inn is located less than one mile from the Great River Route trail. Secure bicycle stowage is available. Since Pat has picked up guests from both the local airport and the marina, he is more than willing to pick up cyclists with his pickup truck if necessary.

The terrain north of Waverly towards Dover is quite hilly, but not nearly as remote as the Missouri segment. The traffic is rather light, with very few big trucks. To the south, between Waverly and Nunnelly, the terrain levels out a bit. It's not flat, but definitely not as hilly as the area to the north of Waverly.

Because of the low population density there are few services along this route. Anyone cycling through this area, in either direction, must pack plenty of water and emergency food supplies. Refill your water bottles at every opportunity.

The nearest full-service bike shops are rather far away, in Clarksville, Nashville, and Franklin, Tennessee; Carbondale, Illinois, and Paducah, Kentucky.

The Richland Road Loop (8 miles) and the Jesse James Loop (27 miles) both give a flavor of the local area. Taking the Richland Loop counterclockwise from the Nolan House will bring you back to the Great River Route several miles north of Waverly and completely avoid all in-town traffic. If staying an extra day in Waverly, the Jesse James Loop is well worth riding. It is historic, scenic, and has very little traffic.

27-mile tour to Jesse James' homestead

0.0   Begin at Nolan House B&B. Proceed south on SR 13
0.3   Right onto US 70 West
11.3   Left onto CR 927 South
14.3   Left onto Old SR 1 East
16.3   Jesse James homestead from 1878-80. *Note:* This is private property. Look but do not enter. Continue on Old SR 1 East.
23.4   Left onto CR 570 North.
25.2   Right onto US 70 East.
26.6   Left onto SR 13 North.
26.9   Finish—Nolan House B&B.

8-mile Richland Road tour

0.0   Begin—Nolan House B&B. Proceed North on SR 13.
0.5   Left onto Fort Hill Rd. Becomes Richland Rd.
3.8   Left onto CR 574.
7.2   Left onto US 70 East.
7.7   Left onto SR 13 North.
8.0   Finish—Nolan House B&B.

Directions to The Nolan House

Upon entering Waverly, both north- and southbounders must turn onto US 70 East for 0.4 miles to TN 13. Turn left onto TN 13 North for 0.4 miles. The Nolan House will be on the left, immediately north of the bridge.

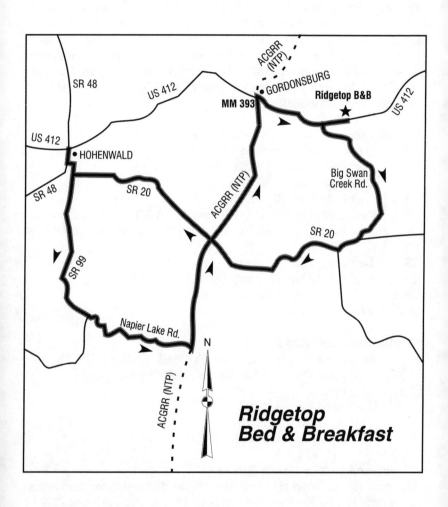

SR 48

US 412

ACGRR (NTP)

GORDONSBURG

Ridgetop B&B

MM 393

US 412

US 412

HOHENWALD

SR 48

SR 20

Big Swan Creek Rd.

ACGRR (NTP)

SR 20

SR 99

SR 20

Napier Lake Rd.

N

ACGRR (NTP)

Ridgetop
Bed & Breakfast

Ridgetop Bed & Breakfast

P.O. Box 193
Highway 412   *AC: GR II, 25*
Hampshire, TN 38461
Bill and Kay Jones, Hosts

RATES :	**Budget - Moderate**
LATITUDE/LONGITUDE:	**N 35 34' 18" W 87 21' 22"**
INTERNET ACCESS:	**Only from main house. There are no phones in the guest cabins.**
WEB SITE:	**www.bbonline.com/ridgetop**
E-MAIL :	**natcheztrace@worldnet.att.net**
RESERVATION INFO:	**(800) 377-2770**

Ridgetop Bed & Breakfast is easily the most remote and rustic inn profiled in this edition of *Bed, Breakfast & Bike*. Set in the midst of 170 acres on a secluded and forested hilltop, the contemporary cedar main house has one guestroom. There are also two delightful guest cottages—a circa 1830 log cabin and a Swiss chalet—on the property. Numerous hiking trails are scattered throughout the property, and if you arrive in mid-July, be prepared to stuff yourself with the juicy blueberries that grow in abundance. Kay will gladly put plenty of them into the breakfast pancakes or muffins served in the main house.

For dinner, the innkeepers recommend the Rio Colorado restaurant in Hohenwald, 12 miles away. But if a rather large group of cyclists arrives late at the inn without a support vehicle, Kay can usually provide a dinner—provided she has fair warning. For small groups or couples, the innkeepers will loan out one of their vehicles for a dinner run into Hohenwald or Columbia, 12 and 21 miles away, respectively.

Cycling from Ridgetop
There are three bike shops in this area: Bicycle Joe's and The Wheel in Columbia, and the awesome Lightning Cycles in Franklin. Included in this book is a rather long figure eight loop

that may be broken into two separate tours along deserted and scenic back roads. Thanks to its isolation, bicycle security is no problem at the Ridgetop Bed & Breakfast.

47-mile Hohenwald Loop

0.0	Begin: entrance to Ridgetop B&B. Proceed West on US 412
0.8	Left onto Big Swan Creek Rd.
7.8	Right onto SR 20
13.8	Cross Natchez Trace Parkway
19.8	Left onto SR99. Hohenwald, TN, will be just to the right of this intersection
25.3	Left onto Napier Lake Rd.
30.3	Left onto Natchez Trace Parkway North
40.2	Exit onto US 412 East
46.7	Finish: entrance to Ridgetop B&B

Directions to Ridgetop

At MM 393 exit onto US 412 East. After two miles, stop off at the Gordonsburg Farm Market and call the Ridgetop. Bill or Kay will either come and shuttle you up the horrendous hill to their inn or leave their pickup truck parked at the Gordonsburg Market to drive yourself. If you really feel like you need an extremely steep climb, then continue on Highway 412 for another two miles after the market. The green and white sign for Ridgetop will be on the left just past MM 27 and Finis Road. If there is a SAG along, do not even think about driving up the front hill; instead, take the back road. If you are coming off the Trace onto 412 East, the SAG should go 2.5 miles and turn left onto Ridgetop Road. for 2.5 miles to the green and white Ridgetop B&B sign on the right.

Riverfront Plantation Inn

190 Crow Lane
Dover, TN 37058   *AC: GR II, 21*
Fulton & Lynn Combs, Hosts

RATES :	**Moderate**
LATITUDE/LONGITUDE:	**N36 29' 25" W 87 50' 42"**
INTERNET ACCESS:	**From the common area**
WEB SITE:	**www.riverfrontplantation.com**
E-MAIL:	**flcombs@ibm.net**
RESERVATION INFO:	**(931) 232-9492**
FAX:	**(931) 232-5267**

One would never guess that the splendidly restored Riverfront Plantation Inn was once squarely in the middle of a major Civil War battle. Immediately adjacent to a national cemetery and Ft. Donelson, the Riverfront Plantation Inn stood within the defensive works constructed by the rebel army to resist the Union Army led by Ulysses S. Grant in 1862. Due to its location on the battlefield, the house was under constant bombardment by Union artillery and small arms, the remains of which constantly pop up to the surface on the lawn and surrounding fields, particularly after a heavy rainfall. Over the years, innkeeper Fulton Combs has collected enough artifacts to turn the inn into a showcase of Civil War memorabilia. He also has one of the few collections of Civil War artillery projectiles in the country.

Shortly after the battle, the house was further damaged by fire; what remained was utilized by the U.S. forces as a field hospital. This probably accounts for the sightings of blue-clad Union soldiers in the back bedroom. There have been several instances of items falling and breaking for no apparent reason. Lynn often hears footsteps when the house is empty.

The Georgian-style mansion is perched high on a bluff with a splendid view of the Cumberland River valley below. In addition to Civil War-related paintings, artifacts, and wall coverings, the five cheerfully decorated, king-sized guestrooms have modern furnishings and an enclosed screened-in porch. A complimentary gift basket and refreshments are served upon arrival. Coffee, pastries, and a newspaper are delivered to the guestrooms in the morning. Later, a full plantation breakfast is served on a sun-drenched, air-conditioned porch, with flocks of hummingbirds buzzing around the outside feeders.

Breakfast is prepared in a commercial-grade kitchen, where Lynn also produces lunches and dinners for B&B guests as well as for wedding receptions and banquets. If you're looking for a quick bite, there are several fast food restaurants in the village. The B&M diner on Highway 70 just east of the village center serves excellent milk shakes.

Cycling from Riverfront Plantation Inn

The northbound terrain along the Land Between the Lakes (LBL) Parkway moderates a bit. However, there are no grocery stores or accommodations of any sort except for campgrounds on the LBL Parkway. If continuing southbound towards Waverly, Tennessee, be prepared for remote, backcountry roads with severe hills. Take plenty of water and extra rations in either direction. Except for US 70, which has a wide, paved shoulder, there is very light traffic along the Great River Route both north and south of Dover.

With pre-arrangement, Fulton Combs will shuttle bikes between the LBL and the inn. Secure bicycle stowage is available.

The nearest bike shops are:

> Van Camps Bicycle Shop (30 miles away)
> 1352 Fort Campbell Boulevard
> Clarksville, TN 37042
> (931) 645-4858

Bikes and Moore (35 miles away)
200 Sivley Road
Hopkinsville, KY 42240
(270) 885-0613

Bicycle Center of Clarksville (35 miles away)
1450 Madison Street
Clarksville, TN 37040
(931) 647-2453

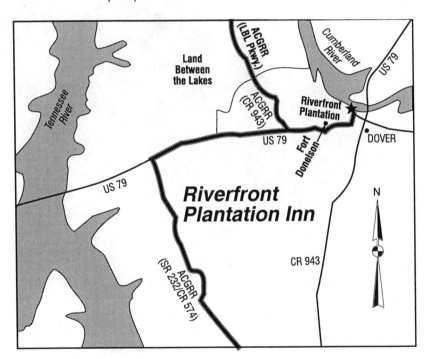

Directions to Riverfront Plantation Inn

The inn is four miles east of the intersection of the LBL Parkway and US 79. After passing the entrance to Ft. Donelson (on the left), be prepared for a long downhill coast before making a left turn at the bottom onto Church Street, followed by a short climb. Just a few hundred feet beyond, turn left following the sign to the cemetery. The road to the inn, just to the right of the cemetery entrance, is marked with a large sign.

From 1878 until 1880, this farm near Waverly, Tennessee, was rented by Jesse James under the alias of J.D. Howard. Locals called him "The Rabbit Man," because he was perceived as being very timid. To visit the farm, see the bike ride detailed on page 183.

Corrections and Enhancements to the Great River Route

Correction to AC: GR I, 9

(Northbound)
00 (km) Continue on Judith Spring Rd. In 0.2 mi, turn right onto unsigned CR BB.

There are two mistakes here:

1) Continue on Judith Spring Rd. In 2 miles (not 0.2) turn right onto unsigned CR BB.

2) CR BB is now signed at that intersection.

New Roads/St. Francisville/Jackson, Louisiana, to Norwood, Louisiana
AC: GR III, 43 and ST VI, 79

The normal northbound route turns from SR 10 onto SR 421 North just west of Jackson, Mississippi. Personal experience has clearly shown that the bridge on Core Road (which crosses Thompson Creek about eight miles to the north) has been known to be washed away during flooding. It also has a skimpy nine-foot clearance and a rather low weight limit. Thus, any riders being accompanied by a heavy SAG (Supplies and Gear) vehicle might find it impossible to get the SAG across that bridge. In contrast, the suggested modification runs through the bicycle-friendly village of Jackson, Louisiana, home of two very good B&B inns (the Old Centenary Inn and the Millbank House) plus a nice restaurant, Bear's Corners.

Northbound: Continue east on Highway 10 for less than a mile through Jackson. Everything of interest, including both B&Bs

and the Bear's Corners restaurant, will be on the right hand (south side) of the highway. Turn left onto Highway 952 North. Shortly after making this turn you pass by the West Florida Historical Museum run by Earl Smith (earl256@hotmail.com), a cyclist and member of the Baton Rouge Bicycle Club. Earl has offered to touring cyclists the use of the museum facilities, including camping on the grounds. If nothing else, stop in, fill your water bottles, and say hello.

Continue northbound on Highway 952 for 12 miles to the intersection with SR 68. Continue straight onto Highway 68 into the hamlet of Wilson. As the road enters Wilson it will turn sharply to the left. At the stop sign, continue straight onto the Old Wilson-Norwood Road for about four miles into Norwood. Once in Norwood, turn right, cross the railroad and then left onto Highway 19 North. About half a mile north of Norwood you will pass Thompson Creek Road on the left, which is the original Adventure Cycling route. Continue on Highway 19 North into Mississippi. For northbounders, Norwood LA is barely two miles south of the Mississippi state line, where SR 19 becomes MS 33. Regardless of the designation, it is a busy highway with more trucks than cars, thus requiring heightened caution. Fortunately, the Great River Route turns off this busy highway onto Goulden Road East less than than two miles north of the state line.

Southbound: After crossing into Louisiana, continue straight on Highway 19 into Norwood bypassing Thompson Creek Road. At Norwood, turn right over the railroad and then left onto Haynes Road, which parallels the tracks. This road will shortly become the Old Wilson-Norwood Road. Continue on this road into Wilson. Continue straight at the stop sign and follow the road—now Highway 68—around to the right to the intersection with CR 952. Continue straight onto Highway 952 for 12 miles into Jackson and the intersection with SR 10. As you enter Jackson note the West Florida Historical Museum on the left. The Museum Director, Earl Smith, is a member of the Baton Rouge Bicycle Club and has opened his facilities, including camping on the grounds, to touring cyclists. Turn right onto Highway 10 West through

Jackson. About half a mile west of Jackson you will arrive at the intersection of SR 10 & 421. From that point the original Adventure Cycling southbound route continues towards St. Francisville.

For southbounders, a rather big decision is looming. If headed into Baton Rouge just follow the Adventure Cycling Baton Rouge spur south on US 61. However, if you want to continue on into New Orleans, avoiding Baton Rouge in the process, follow the AC directions into St. Francisville to the intersection of SR 10, Ferdinand and Commerce Streets. Continue on SR 10 West to the St. Francisville ferry. Once in New Roads, merely reverse the northbound directions through Grosse Tete and Plaquemine into New Orleans.

Natchez, Mississippi, to the Natchez Trace Parkway
AC: GR III, 41

Following is the recommended route from Natchez to the Natchez Trace Parkway (NTP), avoiding US 61. Refer to the AC map and the map on page 139.

Northbound
0.0	Begin at intersection of US 61, Devereau Dr. & Lynda Lee Dr. Proceed on Lynda Lee North.
0.7	Turn right onto SR 555 (ML King Jr.)
6.0	Easy right onto SR 554 (Airport Rd.) Avoid the hard right onto Foster Mound Rd.
10.0	Left onto Artman Rd.
12.7	Right onto McGehee Rd.
14.6	Follow pavement to the left onto Emerald Mound Rd.
15.8	Straight onto SR 553 for just a few yards to the NTP. Turn left onto the NTP North.

Note: If northbound towards Jim's Cabin Rental at Church Hill, turn left onto SR 553 North for seven miles. Jim's property will be on the right directly opposite the large church.

Southbound from the NTP

0.0	At NTP MM 10 turn right onto SR 553. Continue straight onto Emerald Mound Rd.
1.2	Follow pavement right onto McGehee Rd.
3.1	Left onto Artman Rd. South.
5.8	Turn right onto CR 554 West.
9.8	Easy left onto SR 555 (ML King Jr) South
15.2	Left onto Wilson Rd. (becomes Lynda Lee)
15.8	Finish—intersection of US 61, Devereau Dr. & Lynda Lee Dr. To continue south on the GRR, go straight through intersection and bear right onto US 61 South.

Jackson, Mississippi
AC GR Route III, 37 & 38

In addition to being burned to the ground by General U.S. Grant, Jackson, Mississippi represents a major break in the NTP (no connection). At presstime, it stops at Ridgeland on the north side of Jackson and starts again near Clinton southwest of Jackson. The original Jackson Bypass had serious problems, particularly along County Line Road, a narrow thoroughfare with heavy truck traffic. Fortunately, an improved bypass has taken care of the County Line Road segment, while, in the long term, completion of the NTP around Jackson is currently underway and could be done in 2002. In the meantime, one still has the option of going around Jackson via the enhanced bypass or cycling through mid-city. Both options have their advantages. Assistance with both was provided by Jim Parks, Emeritus Librarian at Millsaps College (parksjf@millsaps.edu).

In addition to very nice bed & breakfast inns, camping is also a possibility in the Jackson area at Le Fleurs Bluff State Park. For info on Jackson accommodations, contact the Visitors Bureau at (800) 354- 7695.

Southbound Bypass

0.0	Start at the intersection of US 51 & the NTP access road. Turn right onto Hwy 51 North.
0.3	Left onto West Jackson. After 0.7 miles, bear right and then after less than 0.1 mile bear left onto Old Agency to

pass under I-55. Just 0.2 miles beyond the interstate you will encounter Highland Colony Parkway.

1.5   Left onto Highland Colony Parkway. This is a rather new road, much favored by the local cycling community.

5.5   Right onto County Line for about 0.1 mile and then left onto the Echelon Parkway to the T intersection with Watkins Dr.

6.3   Left onto Watkins Dr. and then, after just a few yards, turn right onto Livingston Rd. After about half a mile Livingston will bear Left.

7.3   Right onto Beasley Rd.

9.0   After crossing the tracks, turn right onto Hilda Dr.

10.5   Left onto County Line Rd. West for less than 0.2 miles and then turn left onto Cynthia.

12.0   Cross US 49.

15.0   Left onto Northside Dr.

16.6   Left onto Cynthia St.

17.0   Left onto Monroe St.

17.9   Right onto West College.

18.3   Left onto West Madison.

18.6   Pass under I-20. This represents the end of the enhanced southbound Jackson bypass.

To regain the NTP, continue straight for just a few yards past the interstate and turn right onto Frontage Road West for a little over one mile.

Northbound Bypass

0.0   Start at the intersection of I-20 and West Madison.

0.3   Right onto West College.

0.7   Left onto Monroe St.

1.6   Right onto Cynthia St.

2.0   Right onto Northside Dr.

3.6   Left onto Cynthia Rd.

6.6   Cross US 49.

8.0   Right onto West County Line Rd., then right onto Hilda Dr.

9.7   Left onto Beasley Rd.

11.4   Left onto Livingston. After 0.4 miles bear right onto Livingston Rd.

12.4   Left onto Watkins Dr. and after a few yards right onto the Echelon Pky.

13.1   Right onto County Line and then left onto Highland Colony Pky.

17.1   Right onto Old Agency Rd. and pass under I-55. Then right onto Sunnybrook Rd. and then left onto West Jackson.

18.4   Right onto US 51.

18.6   Left onto the access road to the Mississippi Arts & Crafts Center and NTP.

Jackson Mid-City Route

Southbound

0.0   Start at the intersection of US 51 and the NTP access road. Proceed south on US 51.

8.3   Left onto Fairview Ave. Shortly after making that turn, the Fairview Inn will be the imposing structure on your left. To reach the Millsaps Buie House continue south on State St. (US 51).

9.0   Pass through intersection of State St. (US 51) and Fortification. This will be the turnoff point for continuing on to the Clinton end of the NTP. To reach the Milsaps Buie House continue straight on State St. for half a mile. It will be on the left. If continuing through Jackson turn right onto Fortification St. West. Remain on this street as it goes through its various incarnations of Woodrow Wilson and Bullard.

13.3   Bear right onto West Capital. Shortly thereafter, the street passes under I-220 and becomes Clinton Blvd.

18.0   Bear right onto East College.

19.2   Left onto West Madison.

20.2   Finish at intersection of West Madison and I-20.

Northbound

0.0   Start at Intersection of West Madison and I-20. Proceed north on West Madison.

1.0   Right onto West College.

2.4   Left onto Clinton Blvd. After passing under I-220, continue straight for just a few hundred yards on West Capital.

6.2 Bear left onto Bullard, which will become Woodrow Wilson and then Fortification St.

10.5 Intersection of Fortification and High Streets. For the Millsaps Buie House, turn right onto State St. (US 51) for one half mile. The Inn will be on your left. To continue northbound, turn left onto State St. US 51 North.

11.2 For the Fairview Inn, turn right onto Fairview St. Shortly after making that turn, the Fairview Inn will be the imposing structure on your left. If bound for the NTP, continue north on State St. (US 51).

20.2 Finish at intersection of US 51 and the access road to the NTP and the Mississippi Arts & Crafts Center.

The two local bike shops are:

The Bike Rack
2282 Lakeland Dr
Flowood, MS 39208
(601) 936-2100
www.bikerackms.com
bikerack@netdoor.com

Indian Cycle
P.O. Box 1287
125 Dyess Rd
Ridgeland, MS 39157
(601) 956-8383
(800) 898-0019

The Nashville Spur

For north- and southbounders, the Nashville Spur begins at the intersection of SR 50 and MM 408 on the Natchez Trace Parkway. At that point, southbound Great Rivers Route riders coming from Waverly, Tennessee, will turn onto the NTP South. Northbound riders continuing on the Great Rivers Route will turn onto SR 50 West. This intersection also offers free camping with running water but no showers.

Riders continuing on into Nashville must continue north on the NTP. Given the rather unfriendly traffic conditions where the NTP ends at SR 100, I have devised an alternate back roads route from MM 415 through Leipers Fork, the Old Natchez Trace, and Percy Warner Park to the intersection of Belle Meade Boulevard and Harding/West End Road. From that point the route follows a major thoroughfare for about six miles to its end in downtown Nashville. See maps on pages 176 and 179.

Northbound

0.0	Begin at the intersection of SR 50 and MM 408 of the NTP and proceed north on the NTP.
8.2	Exit onto SR 7 East. This pleasant downhill will bring you to Wilson Fly's General Store in Fly, TN, just two miles from the NTP.
11.2	Left onto Leiper's Creek Rd. North.
23.0	Arrive Namasté Acres B&B (see page 177).
25.3	Continue straight onto SR 46 North.
26.4	Pass through hamlet of Leiper's Fork.
31.8	Cross SR 96. Continue straight on SR 46 North.
33.8	Left onto Old Natchez Trace. The designation will change to Ash Grove Ct. and then back to Old Natchez Trace.
38.0	Right onto Sneed Rd.
38.5	Left onto Vaughn Rd.
40.7	Cross Old Hickory Blvd. (SR 254) and continue straight into Percy Warner Park. The road will turn to gravel for about one half mile.
41.2	Turn right onto one-way Park Loop Road and prepare yourself for severe ups and downs.
48.0	After exiting the park, continue straight onto Belle Meade Blvd.
51.0	Right onto US 70 North, Harding Rd.
55.5	Cross I-40. Continue straight on US 70 North which now becomes West End Ave. and finally Broadway Ave.
56.5	Finish—intersection of US 70 and 1st Ave. in downtown Nashville.

Southbound

0.0	Begin at intersection of US 70 and 1st Ave. in downtown Nashville.
1.0	Cross I-40. Continue straight on US 70 South which becomes Harding Rd.
5.5	Left onto Belle Meade Blvd.
8.5	Continue straight into Percy Warner Park and right onto the one-way Park Loop Rd.
13.6	Right onto a gravel road.
14.0	Cross Old Hickory Blvd. (SR 254) and continue straight onto Vaughn Rd.
16.2	Right onto Sneed Rd.
16.7	Left onto Old Natchez Trace.
20.9	Right onto SR 46 South.
24.0	Cross SR 96 and continue straight on SR 46 South.
29.4	Pass through hamlet of Leiper's Fork.
30.5	Continue straight onto Leiper's Creek Rd.
32.8	Arrive Namasté Acres (see page 177). Continue south on Leiper's Creek Rd.
44.6	Right onto SR 7.
47.1	Left onto NTP South.
55.5	Finish—intersection of SR 50 and MM 408 of the NTP. If bound for Natchez, MS, continue south on the NTP. If bound for St. Louis, MO, turn onto SR 50 West.

Note: The one-mile discrepancy between the Northbound and Southbound Spurs is due to the slightly different route through Percy Warner Park.

Labadie, Missouri
AC GR I, 9

At presstime, the above-noted Adventure Cycling map directs the northbound rider to continue on Old Highway 100 and turn left onto CR T at mile 7.5.

Recommended enhancement:

Northbound: At mile 4.0 bear left onto Dunn Springs Road. If bound for the Staats-Waterford Estate, turn left onto the Boles Road for about 0.3 miles. The Staats-Waterford Estate will be on the right. If not stopping at the Staats-Waterford Estate, continue straight on the Dunn Springs/Boles Road. At mile 5.8, turn left onto CR T and you will have rejoined the original Great Rivers Route.

Southbound: After passing under the Labadie railroad trestle, continue on CR T West for 2.2 miles. Turn right onto the Boles Road. If bound for Washington, Missouri, continue straight onto the Dunn Springs Road. After 1.8 miles, bear right onto Old Highway 100 West. If bound for the Staats-Waterford Estate, follow Boles Road around to the right for about 0.3 miles. The Staats-Waterford Estate will be on the right.

The Marquardt Trail

The Marquardt Trail, named after retired farmer Paul Marquardt of Prairie du Rocher, Illinois, offers a flat and scenic alternative route into St. Louis, avoiding the dangerous hills along the Great Rivers Route between Cape Girardeau, Missouri, and St. Louis.

Northbound

0.0	Begin at the intersection of CR 6 & Shawneetown Trail (Ft. Gage). Proceed north on CR 6. *Map Reference:* TAT: X, 113.
5.5	After passing through the village of Ellis Grove, turn left onto SR 3 North.
6.0	Left onto Root Rd.; becomes CR 7 (Bluff Rd.)
17.7	In the village of Prairie du Rocher, turn right onto SR 155 North. This is the location of the Maison du Rocher.
17.9	Left onto CR 7/Bluff Rd.
31.0	At intersection of CR 3 and 855 turn left to remain on CR 3/Bluff Rd. If bound for the Corner George Inn, turn right onto CR 855 for two miles to Maeystown, IL.
37.6	Upon the site of old Valmeyer, CR 3 turns sharply left to

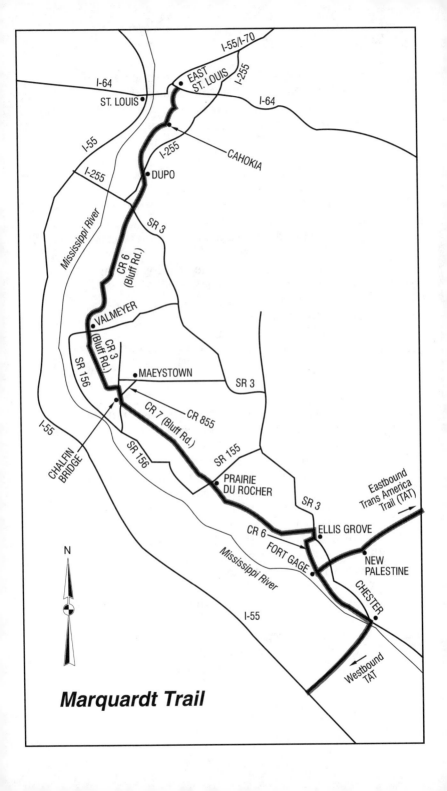

Marquardt Trail

join SR 156. Continue straight over the RR and then right onto CR 6 North. *Note:* Since there are no street signs, this turn is *very* easy to bypass. If you miss this turn you will end up back in Prairie du Rocher.

52.3 Cross under SR 3 and make the first left and then left again to remain on old SR 3.

55.9 Cross over I-255 onto Main St. in Dupo. Remain on Main St. North, keeping the RR to the left.

58.1 In north Dupo, turn left and cross RR onto Water St. Remain on Water St. into Cahokia.

60.0 Cross SR 3 and one block later turn left onto Church St. Follow it north to East 1st St. Turn right and then left to cross SR 157. Street becomes Falling Springs Rd.

61.0 Bear right onto Upper Cahokia Rd.

63.7 Left onto Piggot St. North.

64.0 Right onto 17th East.

64.6 Left onto Broadway North.

66.0 Finish—East St. Louis Metro station at 4th and Broadway.

Southbound

0.0 Begin at the East St. Louis Metro station at the intersection of 4th and Broadway. Proceed south on Broadway.

1.14 Turn right onto 17th St. West.

1.7 Turn left onto Piggot St. South.

2.0 Right onto S. 20th St.—becomes Upper Cahokia Rd.

4.7 Straight onto Falling Springs Rd.

5.2 Cross SR 157 and then right onto East 1st St.

5.3 Left onto Church St. South.

5.6 Right onto East 5th St. and cross SR 3. After crossing SR 3 bear left onto Water St.

6.9 Cross the Cahokia Canal. Remain on Water St. through North Dupo.

7.5 After crossing the RR, turn right onto N. Main, which will become South Main.

9.6 Pass through Dupo.

10.2 Pass over I-255 and bear right to remain on old SR 3.

13.3 Bear left to remain on old SR 3.

13.6   Bear left and then right to rejoin Old SR 3. Turn right towards SR 3.

13.8   Cross under SR 3 and continue straight onto CR 6.

28.5   Left onto SR 156 at the T intersection in old Valmeyer. After crossing the RR, easy right onto West Miller (due to the floods, the street signs are mostly gone) which will turn sharply to the right and become CR 3 (Bluff Rd.).

35.2   Pass through hamlet of Chalfin Bridge. Bluff Rd. makes a sharp left and then a right to become CR 7. If bound for the Corner George B&B, remain straight on CR 855 for about two miles into Maeystown, otherwise make the right turn to remain on Bluff Rd. South towards Prairie du Rocher.

48.3   Right onto SR 155 and enter Prairie du Rocher.

48.5   Left to remain on Bluff Rd. (CR 7). The Maison du Rocher will be off to the right on Duclos St. just one block after making this left turn.

52.9   Shortly after passing through the hamlet of Modoc, bear left to remain on CR 7 South, which will become Root Rd.

61.0   Right onto SR 3.

61.5   Right onto CR 6 and pass through hamlet of Ellis Grove.

66.0   Finish Marquardt Trail at intersection of CR 6 and Shawneetown Trail (Ft. Gage). From this point, the westbound Trans America Trail (TAT) continues south on CR 6 towards the Chester bridge. The eastbound TAT continues along Shawneetown Rd. towards New Palestine. You will need maps 113-117, section 10, of the TAT.

Vicksburg Side Trip

The Vicksburg Side Trip should be included on any Natchez Trace trip. This 55-mile side trip may be easily divided onto two segments of 33 miles (Jackson to Vicksburg) and 22 miles (Vicksburg to MM 59 on the Natchez Trace Parkway).

The terrain is definitely up and down. There are no killer hills in the countryside, but Vicksburg itself is another matter. In addition to some bad hills, the traffic is rather unyielding. Traffic is minimal on Old US 80 between Clinton and Vicksburg, but a bit heavier south of Vicksburg along Halls Ferry/Fisher Ferry Road.

Southbound—Jackson to Vicksburg and return to the NTP

0.0	Start at intersection of NTP MM 87 and Frontage Rd. Proceed West on Frontage Rd. This road endures various incarnations, such as Frontage Rd., Old US 80, Madison St., SR 467. Regardless of the designation, remain on this road all the way to Bovina. At Edwards, turn left and then shortly thereafter bear right to remain on Old US 80.
20.3	At Bovina turn left to remain on old Hwy. 80 and shortly thereafter turn right at the T to Bovina Dr.
20.4	Left to remain on Bovina Dr. to Warrior Trail.
20.6	Right onto Warrior Trail.
24.1	Bear right under the RR trestle and then left to remain on Warrior Trail.
25.1	Re-cross the tracks and continue straight on Warrior Trail West. Ignore the right-hand turn onto Warrior which will pop up about 0.2 miles after crossing the tracks.
26.1	Right onto Stenson Rd.
27.4	Cross SR 27.
27.9	Right onto Old SR 27.
30.0	Cross I-20, continue straight, then bear right onto Clay St.
30.3	Left onto Clay St. West—a very busy road. Immediately after this turn, the Vicksburg Military Park will be on the right. If bound for The Corners B&B, continue on Clay St. West. Prepare yourself for heavy traffic, hills, and rather unpleasant conditions for the next two miles.
32.3	Left onto Washington St. South.

33.0   Right onto Klein St. West and The Corners B&B. *Caution!* When turning onto Klein Street be prepared for a breath-taking—almost vertical—drop. If you are riding a heavily-laden bike, it is suggested that you dismount and walk the bike half way down the hill to the entrance of The Corners on the right. To continue southbound towards the NTP, turn left onto Oak St. South.

34.3   At the end of Oak St., bear right onto Washington St. South.

34.8   Left onto N. Frontage Rd.

36.2   Right onto Hall's Ferry Rd. South, which eventually becomes Fisher Ferry Rd.

55.4   Right onto the NTP South MM 59.

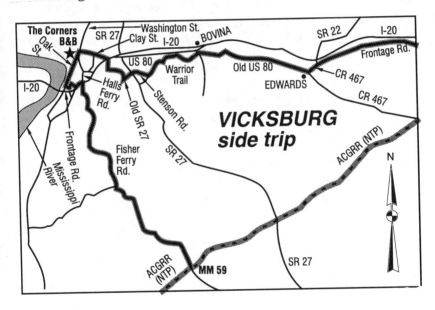

Northbound—NTP to Vicksburg and continuing on to Jackson

0.0   Start at MM 59. Proceed left onto Fisher Ferry Rd. North, which becomes Hall's Ferry Rd.

19.2   Shortly after crossing I-20, left onto N. Frontage Rd. West.

20.6   Right onto Washington St. North.

21.1   Bear left onto Oak St.

22.4   Arrive at The Corners B&B at the corner of Oak and Klein Streets. Upon departing the Corners, turn left up the hill to Washington St. Turn left onto Washington St. North.

23.1   Right onto Clay.

25.1   Shortly after passing Union St. on the right, turn right onto the next unnamed road, which will eventually become Old SR 27. After less than 0.3 miles, bear left to cross I-20 and continue straight on old SR 27.

27.2   Left onto Stenson Rd.

28.5   Left at T onto Warrior Trail East.

29.4   Bear onto the easy right to remain on Warrior Trail. Shortly thereafter, cross the train tracks and bear right.

30.6   Turn right under the RR trestle and then left to remain on Warrior Trail East.

34.3   Left onto Bovina Dr. North. After 0.2 to 0.3 miles, bear right to remain on Bovina for another 0.1 mile.

34.6   Left onto Old US 80. Shortly thereafter, at the intersection of US 80, bear right onto Old US 80.

42.4   At Edwards, the road jogs to the left and then back to the right again. Remain on Old US 80, which will be variously designated as Frontage Rd, SR 467, and Madison St. (in Bolton).

50.2   Pass through Bolton. Continue straight on East Madison, which again becomes Old US 80.

55.4   Finish at the NTP underpass.

If continuing northbound on the Natchez Trace Parkway, remain on Frontage Road and follow the directions to the Jackson Bypass or Mid-City Route on page 194.

Appendix: Bicycle Shops
and Bicycle-Friendly Addresses Along the Great Rivers Route and Alternates

Alabama

Florence

Gusmus Bike Shop
322 North Poplar Street
Florence, AL 35330
(256) 764-3412

Sheffield

Bikes Plus
3928 Jackson Highway
Sheffield, AL 35660
(256) 381-2453

Illinois

Carbondale

Bike Surgeon
302 West Walnut
Carbondale, IL 62901
(618) 457-4521

Carbondale Cycle Shop
303 South Illinois Avenue
Carbondale, IL 62901
(618) 549-6863

Phoenix Cycles
300 South Illinois Avenue
Carbondale, IL 62901
(618) 549-3612

Fairview Heights

Touring Cyclist
4632 North Illinois Street
Fairview Heights, IL 62208
(618) 233-8181

Kentucky

Paducah

Bike World
848 Joe Clifton Drive
Paducah, KY 42001
(502) 442-0751

Hoopers Outdoor Center
3791 Hinkleville Road
Paducah, KY 42001
(270) 442-7816

Toys R US
5015 Hinkleville Road
Paducah, KY 42001
(270) 575-3336

Louisiana

Ferry Schedules

www.dotd.state.la.us/about/ferry/schedule.shtml

Baton Rouge

Tuffy's
257 Lee Drive
Baton Rouge, LA 70802
(225) 766-2453

Capitol Cyclery
8424 Florida Boulevard
Baton Rouge, LA 70802
(225) 927-1997

The Bicycle Shop
3315 Highland Road
Baton Rouge, LA 70802
(225) 344-5624

Gonzales

The Bicycle Connection
108 East Ascension Street
Gonzales, LA 70737
(225) 647-9352.

Jackson

Feliciana Chamber of Commerce
P.O. Box 667
Jackson, LA 70748
(225) 634-7155
info@felicianatourism.org

Republic of West Florida Historical Museum
Earl Smith, Director
3405 College Street, P.O. Box 1000
Jackson, LA 70748
(225) 634-7155
earl56@hotmail.com
http://atos.stirlingprop.com/jackson/

New Orleans

Adams Bicycle World
3146 Calhoun Street
New Orleans, LA 70125
(504) 861-0032

Bayou Bicycle Inc.
3534 Toulouse Street
New Orleans, LA 70119
(504) 488-1946

Bicycle Michael's
622 Frenchmen Street
New Orleans, LA 70116
(504) 945-9505
Bikemike@aol.com

Bikes Plus
3112 Paris Avenue
New Orleans, LA 70119
(504) 944-6389
cyclists@gnofn.org
http://home.gnofn.org/~cyclists

Crescent City Cyclists
P.O. Box 6095
Metairie, LA 70009-6095
http://home.gnofn.org/~cyclists

French Quarter Bicycles
522 Dumaine Street
New Orleans, LA 70116
(504) 529-3136

GNO Cyclery
1426 South Carrollton Avenue
New Orleans, LA 70118
(504) 861-0023

Michael Hamner
French Louisiana Bike Tours
3216 West Esplanade PMB 302
New Orleans, LA 70116
(800) 346-7989
Fax: (504) 488-9818
www.flbt.com
info@flbt.com
http://freeman.sob.tulane.edu/bike/mikepage.htm
(a great site on cycling in New Orleans)

Herwigs Bicycle Store
5924 Magazine Street
New Orleans, LA 70115
(504) 897-2311

Joe's Lawn Mower and Bicycle
2501 Tulane Avenue
New Orleans, LA 70119
(504) 821-2350

Toys R Us
12250 I-10 Service Road
New Orleans, LA 70128
(504) 245-8697

Triangle Bicycle and Lawnmower Store
5433 Crowder Boulevard
New Orleans, LA 70127
(504) 241-3239

Plaquemine

Gatorland Bike Shop
58945 Belleview Road - State Highway 75
Plaquemine, LA 70764
(225) 687-0212

Missouri

    Cape Girardeau

        Cape Bicycling & Fitness
        2410 William Street
        Cape Girardeau, MO 63701
        (573) 335-2453

    Crystal City

        Crystal City Cyclery
        2292 North Truman Boulevard (Highway 61/67)
        Crystal City, MO 63019
        (314) 937-6201

    Farmington

        Extreme Edge Bicycle Repair Shop
        909 Judy Drive
        Farmington, MO 63640
        (573) 756-4122

    Marquand

        Denny Ward
        121 North Whitener Street
        Marquand, MO 63655
        (573) 783-7525
        dward@mines.missouri.org

    Marthasville

        Scenic Cycles
        Depot Street, P.O. Box 41
        Marthasville, MO 63357
        (636) 433-2909

St. Louis

A&M Cycles
4282 Arsenal Street
St. Louis, MO 63116
(314) 776-1144

A-1 Bicycle Sales & Service
10211 Manchester Road
St. Louis, MO 63122
(314) 821-0214
(314) 821-0216

Bicycle Center
8204 North Broadway
St. Louis MO 63147
(314) 383-3886

Bicycles of Kirkwood
207 North Kirkwood Road
St. Louis, MO 63122
(314) 821-3460

Big Shark Bicycle Company
6681 Delmar Boulevard
St. Louis, MO 63130
(314) 862-1188

Bike & Fitness Center
12011 Manchester Road South
St. Louis, MO 63131
(314) 965-1444

Maplewood Bicycle Sales & Service
7534 Manchester Road
St. Louis MO 63143
(314) 781-9566

Mesa Cycles
1035 South Big Bend Boulevard
St. Louis, MO 63117
(314) 645-4447

Outdoor Exchange & Adventure Co.
7905 Big Bend Boulevard
St. Louis, MO 63119
(314) 962-1823

South County Cyclery Inc
9985 Lin Ferry Drive
St. Louis, MO 63123
(314) 843-5586

South Side Cyclery
6969 Gravois Avenue
St. Louis, MO 63116
(314) 481-1120

Mississippi

Flowood (Jackson)

The Bike Rack
2282 Lakeland Drive
Flowood, MS 39205
(601) 936-2100
www.bikerackms.com
bikerack@netdoor.com

Jackson

LeFleur's Bluff Bicycle Club
P.O. Box 515
Jackson, MS 39205
(601) 372-8949 (Bicycle Hotline)

Paul Hicock
Bicycle Advocacy Group of Mississippi
P.O. Box 515
Jackson MS 39205
hicockp@fiona.umsmed.edu

Natchez

Natchez Bicycling Center
334 Main Street
Natchez, MS 39120
(601) 446-7794

Natchez Convention & Visitors Bureau
422 Main Street
Natchez, MS 39120
(800) 647-0814

Western Auto Associate Store
601 Main Street
Natchez, MS 39120
(601) 445-4186
(800) 647-0814

Ridgeland (Jackson)

Indian Cycle Fitness & Outdoor
1060 East County Line Road
(I-55 North at County Line Road)
Ridgeland, MS 39157
(601) 956-8383
Fax: (601) 956-6230

Tupelo

The Bicycle Shop
Mike Olmstead
1143 West Main Street
Tupelo, MS 38801
(601) 842-7341

The Bicycle Paceline
Brian Piaza
2120 West Jackson Street
Tupelo, MS 38801
*(If southbound, West Jackson is the first overpass
south of the McCollough Boulevard exit. Northbound,
it is the first overpass north of the Main Street exit.)*
(601) 844-8660
Home phone: (662) 841-2556
bicyclep@tsixroads.com

Superintendent
2680 Natchez Trace Parkway
Tupelo, MS 38801-9718
(800) 305-7417
www.nps.gov/natr or www.nps.gov/natt
Emergencies: (800) 300-7275

Tupelo Visitor Center
P.O. Box 1485
Tupelo, MS 38802-1485
(601) 841-6521
(800) 533-0611

Tennessee

Columbia

Bicycle Joe's
2019 South Main Street B
Columbia TN 38401
(931) 381-5706

The Wheel
11 Public Square
Columbia TN 38401
(615) 381-3225

Franklin

Franklin Bicycle Co.
112 Watson Glen
Franklin, TN 37064
(615) 790-2702

Lightning Cycles
Pat Cox, Owner
120 4th Avenue South
Franklin, TN 37064
(615) 794-6050
www.lightningcycles.com

Memphis

Mississippi River Trail
7777 Walnut Grove Road, Box 27
Memphis, TN 38120
(901) 753-1400
www.bicyclemrt.org

Nashville

The Bike Pedlar
2910 West End Avenue
Nashville, TN 37203
(615) 329-2453

Cumberland Transit
2807 West End Avenue
Nashville, TN 37203
(615) 327-4093

Nashville Bicycle Club
P.O. Box 158593
Nashville, TN 37215
www.coolcats.com/nbc.

The Ski Mogul
73 White Bridge Road #G-4
Nashville TN 37205
(615) 356-7669

National cycling-related organizations

Adventure Cycling Association
150 East Pine Street
P.O. Box 8308
Missoula, MT 59807
(800) 755-2453
(406) 721-1776
www.adventurecycling.org
acabike@adv-cycling.org

League of American Bicyclists (LAB)
1612 K Street NW
Suite 401
Washington DC 20006-2082
(202) 822-1333
Fax: (202) 822-1334
www.bikeleague.org
bikeleague@bikeleague.org

Ken Kifer's Bike Pages
www.kenkifer.com

Ed Noonan's Voyager
www.voyager.net/tailwinds